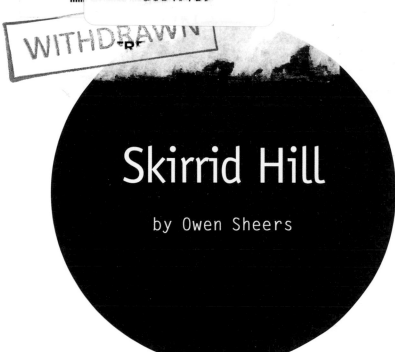

Skirrid Hill

by Owen Sheers

Luke McBratney

Series Editors:
Nicola Onyett and Luke McBratney

HODDER
EDUCATION
AN HACHETTE UK COMPANY

With thanks to Owen Sheers

The publisher would like to thank the following for permission to reproduce copyright material:

Acknowledgements:

Throughout: extracts from *Skirrid Hill* by Owen Sheers. Published by Seren Books, 2005. Copyright © Owen Sheers. Reproduced by permission of the author c/o Rogers, Coleridge & White Ltd., 20 Powis Mews, London W11 1JN; **p.vii: T.S.Eliot:** from 'East Coker', *Four Quartets* (Faber & Faber, 1940) By permission of Faber and Faber Ltd.; **p.7: Sarah Crown:** from 'Parting of the ways (and other dislocations)', (The *Guardian*, 25 February 2006), https://www.theguardian.com/books/2006/feb/25/featuresreviews.guardianreview28, Copyright Guardian News & Media Ltd 2016, reprinted with permission; **p.23: Philip Larkin:** from 'The Trees', *The Collected Poems* (Faber & Faber, 1970) By permission of Faber and Faber Ltd.; **p.85: Seamus Heaney:** from 'The Toome Road', *New Selected Poems 1966–1987* (Faber & Faber, 1979) By permission of Faber and Faber Ltd.

Every effort has been made to trace all copyright holders, but if any have been inadvertently overlooked the Publishers will be pleased to make the necessary arrangements at the first opportunity.

Photo credits:

p.3 © Ian Nellist / Alamy Stock Photo; **p.11** © Sputnik / TopFoto; **p.16** Æ 2005, Digital image, The Museum of Modern Art, New York / Scala, Florence; **p.22** © Robert Read / Alamy Stock Photo; **p.26** © 2006 Keystone / TopFoto; **p.37** © moonrun / Fotolia; **p.39** © Trinity Mirror / Mirrorpix / Alamy Stock Photo; **p.40** © Blickwinkel / Alamy Stock Photo; **p.49** © Mac Adams; **p.52** © PA Photos / TopFoto; **p.56** © Archives du 7e Art / Photos 12 / Alamy Stock Photo; **p.75** © GL Portrait / Alamy Stock Photo

Orders: please contact Bookpoint Ltd, 130 Milton Park, Abingdon, Oxon OX14 4SB. Telephone: (44) 01235 827720. Fax: (44) 01235 400454. Lines are open 9.00–17.00, Monday to Saturday, with a 24-hour message answering service. Visit our website at www.hoddereducation.co.uk

© Luke McBratney 2017

First published in 2017 by

Hodder Education
An Hachette UK Company,
Carmelite House, 50 Victoria Embankment
London EC4Y 0DZ

Impression number	5	4	3	2	1
Year	2021	2020	2019	2018	2017

Cover photo (and throughout) © PsychoShadowMaker/iStock/Thinkstock/Getty Images

Typeset in 11/13pt Univers LT Std 47 Light Condensed by Integra Software Services Pvt. Ltd., Pondicherry, India

Printed in Italy

A catalogue record for this title is available from the British Library

ISBN 9781471853982

Contents

Using this guide

The purposes of this AS/A-level Literature Guide are to enable you to organise your thoughts and responses to the poems by Sheers, to deepen your understanding and enjoyment of them and to help you to address the assessment requirements in order to obtain the best possible grade.

Note that teachers and examiners are seeking above all else evidence of an informed personal response to the text. A guide such as this can help you to understand the text, form your own opinions, and suggest areas to think about, but it cannot replace your own ideas and responses as an informed and autonomous reader.

How to make the most of this guide

We recommend that you read and study independently before turning to the ideas in this guide. After you have formulated an individual response to a poem, you might like to read the relevant poem commentary; or you might like to read a larger section or all the poems, unsupported, before reading the relevant pages of this guide.

The subsequent chapters take a broader view and are designed to enable you to see connections across the whole collection. 'Themes' focuses on how some of the main concerns are explored throughout the poems; 'The poet's methods' considers poetic techniques.

It is vital that you familiarise yourself with the ways your exam board tests your response to the poems. So, use the specification and the sample assessment materials as your definitive guide to what you need to study and how you are going to be assessed.

Studying Sheers' *Skirrid Hill* for A-level

Bear in mind the sort of questions you are going to face in the examination. You need to check which exam board you are using with your teacher. For AQA Specification A, *Skirrid Hill* is a poetry set text in Section A of the Modern Times option (Paper 2B). Typically, the question quotes or states a viewpoint on the collection, then invites you to examine that view. Alternatively, *Skirrid Hill* may be used as a comparative set text in Section B of Modern Times (Paper 2B). In this case, you are given a viewpoint on an idea or issue relating to the Modern Times option. You compare the significance of this idea or issue and how it is presented in *Skirrid Hill* and your other comparative set text.

For Eduqas, *Skirrid Hill* is a comparative set text for Component 1: Poetry. You study the text alongside *Field Work* by Seamus Heaney. In the exam, you are given a critical viewpoint (typically, a quotation) about poetry. You respond to this view, exploring connections between the work of Sheers and Heaney as you do so.

Studying Sheers for AS-level

If you are taking WJEC (Wales only), you complete two answers on Sheers for the AS Paper. The first question asks you to write critically about a single poem. The second invites you to compare how a theme or idea is explored in both *Skirrid Hill* and in poems from *Field Work* by Seamus Heaney. As part of your preparation, you need to practise analysing each poem as well as comparing themes and ideas that are explored by both Sheers and Heaney. As you do so, you should practise commenting on different viewpoints on the poems. Think of different ways to view each of the poems in class and for yourself as well as making full use of the critical view features throughout this guide.

Key elements

This guide is designed to help you to raise your achievement in your examination response to *Skirrid Hill*. It is intended for you to use throughout your AS/A-level English literature course. It will help as you first study the poems and during your revision.

The following features have been used throughout this guide to help you focus your understanding of the poems:

Context

Context boxes give contextual evidence that relates directly to particular aspects of the text.

Build critical skills

Broaden your thinking about the text by answering the questions in the **Build critical skills** boxes. These help you to consider your own opinions in order to develop your skills of criticism and analysis.

Taking it further ▷▷

Taking it further boxes suggest and provide further background or illuminating parallels to the text.

CRITICAL VIEW

Critical view boxes highlight a particular critical viewpoint that is relevant to an aspect of the main text. This allows you to develop the higher-level skills needed to come up with your own interpretation of a text.

TASK

Tasks are short and focused. They allow you to engage directly with a particular aspect of the text.

Introduction

Skirrid Hill is a rich collection of verse that explores varied themes and ideas and covers a range of subjects drawn from family relationships and experiences of love and relationships, as well as reflections on Wales and national identity and responses to places and people from further afield. This introduction uses the epigraph of *Skirrid Hill* as a springboard for considering the collection as a whole.

An epigraph is a quotation placed at the start of a book which usually casts light on the work to follow, typically by suggesting a major theme or concern. The epigraph is often from a writer whose work has influenced the author. *Skirrid Hill*'s is from T. S. Eliot's 'East Coker' (1940):

> *As we grow older*
>
> *The world becomes stranger, the pattern more complicated*
>
> *Of dead and living.*

At first, this choice might seem odd. Eliot, a notoriously difficult, allusive and intellectually-demanding poet whose heyday was in the period of High Modernism (when literature was arguably at its most experimental and elitist), does not seem an obvious influence on Sheers. Yet, when we consider the epigraph closely, it does provide an introduction to aspects of the poetry in *Skirrid Hill*. 'East Coker' is from *Four Quartets*, one of Eliot's later works and less forbidding to readers than earlier writings such as *The Waste Land* (1922). Philosophical and personal, its speaker also shows a humility that is hard to detect in his earlier work. The epigraph comes from Section V of the poem after Eliot's autobiographical speaker has been addressing the reader, reflecting modestly on his writing career ('twenty years largely wasted') and seeing it as a continuous process of learning and reflecting on how difficult it is to express thoughts and feelings adequately in writing. The epigraph considers the way in which things seem clearer and simpler in youth, but as we age their complications emerge. The strangeness of the world becomes more evident and the 'pattern' – which might be read here as the model or the rules – becomes more complicated. This is true of both living and death. We don't really know how we should live, we don't know what happens to us after we die and we don't know how we should prepare for death.

In *Skirrid Hill*, we might detect a similar mood. Sheers' speakers are often reflective, trying to make sense of the past, whether that be, for example, the past of a romantic relationship such as 'Keyways', or of a linguistic, familial or geographical heritage, such as in 'Inheritance' or 'Skirrid Fawr'. The complexities of life are acknowledged too. From recognising the cruelty of nature in poems like 'Late Spring', the abuses of power or the waste of war in ones like 'Drinking with Hitler' or 'Mametz Wood', *Skirrid Hill* is a collection that is alive to the complications of life. Death, and suffering during life, are also explored. For example, Sheers' speakers reflect on the bravery of those battling with breast cancer ('Amazon'), or the effects of early deaths on those left behind (for example, 'Border Country'). As the Eliot epigraph suggests, there is a sense of the strangeness of life in the poetry of Sheers. This can be seen, for example, in reflections on the speaker's grandfather who produces an egg like a magician's trick in 'The Equation' or on the artist Mac Adams in 'Shadow Man'.

Finally, despite the majority of the poems being accessible lyrics, the collection includes some formally experimental poems, such as the stream-of-consciousness-style 'Service' and the quasi-modernist 'Four Movements in the Scale of Two'.

Target your thinking

- What is your considered personal response to the poem – what do you think are its main concerns or ideas? (**AO1**)
- What other interpretations might you offer? (**AO5**)
- Which are the most important methods used in the poem: how does Sheers use them to shape meaning and create effects? (**AO2**)
- How is the meaning of the poem shaped by your understanding of its contexts? (**AO3**)
- In what ways can you connect the poem's themes, ideas or methods to other poems in the selection, or to your comparative set text? (**AO4**)

'Last Act'

On first reading, this poem is puzzling. It seems to be concerned with speech, theatrical performance and poetry. The poet appears to be poised for a performance, in which he is the speaker and the reader the addressee. What is about to take place is a final act – perhaps the most important, most revealing one of all, in which the poet will perform his poems truthfully. On another, more personal, level the poem might be thought of as an intimate revelation from the speaker to a loved one – someone to whom he has finally grown close enough to share his weaknesses with. The last act might be the act of revealing his stammer by deliberately neglecting to use the strategies used by stammerers to conceal their non-fluency. By so doing the speaker is perhaps making himself vulnerable, but also revealing his true self.

Commentary Depending on how you read the poem, this single verse paragraph might be considered a dramatic monologue or a love poem in the form of an intimate lyric. To read the poem as a dramatic monologue we might consider the speaker as one adopting the persona of an actor about to perform in a play's important final act. The conceit of the poet as actor runs through the poem: the term 'my speech' might be a big speech that the actor has had to learn; the 'gaps' in it might represent those parts unlearned or which were performed less well; 'the silent mouthing O' might make the reader think of the actor's voice exercises before going on stage, or even – for some readers – the 'O' might echo the famous prologue to Shakespeare's *Henry V* in which the actor in the role of chorus draws attention to the artifice of acting and the theatre, referring to the Globe theatre as 'this wooden O'.

The vocabulary of the stage also helps to structure the poem. Anticipation and a sense of occasion are built as we move from the speechlessness of the first part of the poem to the point at which the moment of revelation is about to arrive:

Taking it further ▶

For some poets who stammer, poetry has been a means to fluency. Stammering has also been a motif in the work of other writers. For example, in *The School of Eloquence*, Tony Harrison uses forms of inarticulacy and stammering – exemplified by his Uncle Joe and the Greek orator Demosthenes – to explore a wider need for articulation and political representation. See, for example, 'Wordlists' and 'Them & [uz]' in Tony Harrison, *Selected Poems* (Penguin, 2006).

Taking it further ▶

The King's Speech (2010), directed by Tom Hooper and starring Colin Firth as the king, is the story of George VI's struggle to overcome his stammer. Why not watch this film, or search for some reviews on the internet?

the 'drawing back of the curtain' gives way to the actor 'under the spotlight' poised to bow 'as himself/for the first time all night'.

The conceit seems appropriate for this poem, which is positioned before the epigraph as a prologue to the collection. The poem heightens the reader's sense of anticipation for the work to follow and promises both technical accomplishment and truth. The sense that readers will be hearing the poet 'as himself' prepares us for some personal poems – there are many in the collection – and it reminds us of the intimate nature of the genre of poetry, in which perhaps writer and reader are closest. Unlike drama, where the playwright's words are brought to life through a collaborative process involving a director, actors and others, the poet can deliver his condensed thoughts, unmediated, to the reader's eye and ear.

To think of the poem as a love lyric is an equally fruitful approach. If we do this, we might consider it to be much more autobiographical. Sheers has written about his stammer in the past in poems like 'Stammerer on Scree' in his previous collection, *The Blue Book*, and indeed non-fluency might be considered as a motif that runs throughout *Skirrid Hill* – see, for example, 'Inheritance'. In this case the stutter is explored directly; revealing it could be the final, most intimate act of self-revelation by the speaker to his girlfriend. The 'gaps' in his speech are presented at first as being both visually and aurally unattractive: they are 'like missing teeth/in the face of [his] speech' and they make him sound like a 'stuck record'. This last aural image cleverly reinvents a cliché, since usually someone is likened to a stuck record if he or she is verbose and repeating the same idea. Sheers' usage is actually more accurate. A 'stuck record' keeps repeating the same – often unintelligible – sound in a similar manner to one whose fluency of speech has stuck because of a stammer. The imagery of 'the countdown through the page' enacts the aversion technique whereby the stammerer mentally flicks through a thesaurus to try to find an alternative word to the one which is difficult to enunciate.

Such personal revelation is a brave way to begin a new collection. After Sheers' many successes – his first collection had gone into four printings and his non-fiction work *The Dust Diaries* had won the Welsh Book of the Year Award and been named as a Book of the Year by both the *TLS* and *The New Statesman* – some readers might have expected self-aggrandisement, arrogance or at least a bit of showing off. Instead they are given candour and a disarming display of weakness; the 'bowing' in the penultimate line, as well as being an acknowledgement of acclaim, could be a gesture of respect or even deference to his readership.

The speaker's weakness, paradoxically, shows strength: he is strong enough to reveal himself fully to his loved one. Perhaps, like most of us in the early stages of a relationship, he has presented only his best side to his lover, but now has moved from being 'the actor' to being 'himself/for the first time'. In this way the stutter, rather than impeding communication, might be seen as an aid to intimacy. The poem's tone is conversational, perhaps even gentle and loving. This 'last act' suggests that what will follow is increased closeness and love.

'Mametz Wood'

The speaker reflects on the body parts from dead soldiers that continue to surface around Mametz Wood. He describes the bones, which have been uncovered during ploughing, and considers the battle as having wounded the earth, which is expelling these fragments as part of the healing process.

Considering another recent excavation at which 20 bodies with linked arms were found, the speaker imagines them as if they are in the middle of a dance. The image is a perfect expression of their comradeship, closeness and youth. It also points to the grim absurdity of war.

▲ The memorial to the Welsh soldiers at Mametz Wood

Commentary 'Mametz Wood' is a poem with a strong narrative. It comprises two stories. The first reports on the body parts that have surfaced periodically after ploughing in the years following the war. The second details the discovery of a shallow grave in which the bodies of men with linked arms were found. The poem is also an elegy for the lost lives – one that gives a voice to skeletons with 'absent tongues'.

Each stanza is a tercet – a three-line stanza, which is a common form in *Skirrid Hill*. Using tercets allows Sheers to break up aspects of a story or an idea, and it encourages the reader to focus on the ends of lines and stanzas while still keeping the developing story or idea in mind. Free verse – lines that have no regular metre – also helps to give the reader a sense that the speaker's thoughts and feelings are being expressed naturally and in the moment, rather than being produced to follow predetermined beats.

The first four stanzas form the first part of the poem. The first stanza is a single sentence that announces the subject clearly: 'the wasted young'. These words gain prominence by being placed at the very start of the middle line, after an end-stop and before a **caesura**. The two stanzas that follow form a further sentence that details the parts of the soldiers that have been uncovered. It then imagines their final orders. The fourth stanza is a single sentence that concludes the first part of the poem. In a broader perspective, the earth is personified and the soldiers' remains are considered as 'foreign bodies' symptomatic of widespread wounds to the earth. These foreign bodies are being worked back 'to the surface of the skin' as part of the ongoing process of healing.

The second part of the poem starts with the fifth stanza. 'This morning' is a topic marker announcing a new subject and it moves the action from the non-specific time of the first part of the poem right into the present. The fifth and sixth stanzas describe the discovery of the skeletons that have been linked 'arm in arm' and the perspective moves cinematically, from the longshots of the 'one long grave' and the 'broken mosaic of bone' to the image of skeletons 'mid dance' before finally panning to close-up images of 'boots', 'heads' and 'jaws' which have dropped open.

The final stanza holds this image of the open jaws, allowing the reader to ponder its significance, and the image becomes not just visual, but aural as, paradoxically, we imagine the sounds that have 'slipped from their absent tongues'. The image resonates as 'with this unearthing' remind us of the first stands and its mention of the many discoveries of body parts by farmers during the years since the battle. thus sheers provides a pleasing cyclical effect. it links both stories in the poem: that of the general discovery of body parts and that of the particular discovery of the 20 soldiers. Perhaps by doing so, Sheers encourages us to recognise that his moving account of the 20 men is just one part of a much wider story.

In the collection as a whole, growing up is a significant theme. Here it is addressed by the idea of 'the wasted young'. In contrast to young people of

---

caesura a definite break in the middle of a line of verse; it is usually, but not always, indicated by a punctuation mark.

Taking it further ▷

A DVD of Owen Sheers' programme *Battlefield Poet Keith Douglas* (2011) has been released by Digital Classics. See p.76 for more information on Keith Douglas.

Taking it further ▷

Hear Owen Sheers reading the poem by visiting www.poetryarchive.org and searching for 'Mametz Wood' in the search box. Click on 'Owen Sheers' and a list of his recordings will be displayed.

today who talk of being 'wasted' in the colloquial sense of being drunk, these are young men whose youthful promise has been squandered and who had to grow up fast. Youth is evoked by the images of dancing and singing in the final part of the poem and by the phrase that sends them to their deaths: 'they were told to walk, not run'. It sounds like something said by a schoolteacher, and their inexperience is reinforced by the use of the passive voice and the sense that elders must be obeyed. The **half-rhyme** on 'not run' and 'machine guns' links their deaths to the orders that they followed.

The sheer unexpectedness of death is also evoked. No exact moment of dying is described: just the instants before and the after-effects that are unearthed years later. The final image is gruesome and uncanny; the idea of tongueless skulls singing is disturbing. As well as being macabre, the dropped jaws might remind us of the informal adjective 'jaw-dropping': the idea that they would die so young would have been astonishing to the young men, as it is to us.

Perhaps most astonishing is the waste and Sheers conveys this through images of delicacy and beauty being destroyed. The 'broken mosaic' might remind us of precious Roman ruins; the 'bird's egg' metaphor turns the hard bone of a soldier's skull into an image of fragility. Both the egg and the chit (which usually means a brief note such as a bill, but in this case refers to a shoot such as the one which sprouts from the eye of a potato) are images of early stages of development. It is wasteful that these soldiers' lives have been cut off before maturity.

The natural world, often a source of comfort in Sheers' work, seems to have been undermined by a military subtext. The earth is personified as a soldier standing 'sentinel' – possibly one whose previous work has been ineffective – who must now try to deal with the memories of the destruction that took place on his previous watch. The woods are no longer a place of leisure, but a source of danger: they conceal 'nesting machine guns'. The adjective 'nesting' reminds us of the 'blown/and broken bird's egg' in the previous stanza, whose plosive alliteration carries an echo of the explosions of war.

'The Farrier'

A farrier shoes horses. This poem depicts the farrier as an expert who is gentle and at one with the animal on which he works. It details each part of the process – from donning an apron to watching the horse walk off newly shod.

Commentary A vignette of a typical country event, the poem reads like a documentary of a master craftsman at work. It is comprised of eight tercets and a final single line. Each tercet captures a detail of the process.

The first two stanzas, which form a single sentence, describe calm preparation. Images of the farrier smoking in the first three stanzas help convey his patience as well as the unhurried nature of his work. He places a 'roll-up' in his mouth in the first stanza; we see its 'smoke slow-turning' in the second; then we note its smell in the third. The fourth and fifth stanzas detail the farrier's actions as he takes the mare's leg and positions its hoof between his knees.

half-rhyme an aural effect in which words almost, but not entirely, rhyme.

Taking it further ▶

Research *danse macabre* (e.g. on Wikipedia). In what ways might understanding this allusion contribute to your understanding of 'Mametz Wood' and its depiction of death?

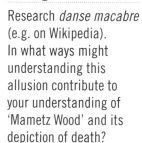

Context

Unlike in many parts of England, where equestrian pursuits are largely the preserve of the wealthy, in Wales, where Sheers grew up, it was not uncommon for someone with a smallholding (a house and some land smaller than a farm) to keep horses.

5

The sixth stanza marks a shift in pace as the farrier carries on with 'the close work' briskly; the speed is enacted by the profusion of dynamic verbs in the space of three lines as he goes to work 'cutting … excavating … filing … and branding on a shoe'. The penultimate stanza provides the conclusion of the shoeing process. Its final line might be seen as a subtle shift in the narrative as we move from the work of the man to the feelings of the horse, who is 'awkward in her new shoes' which alter her perception, making her feel as though she is 'walking on strange ground'. The final stanza deviates from the established stanzaic form by being a single line, making the effects of the shoeing stand out: 'The sound of his steel, biting at her heels.' The formal prominence is highlighted aurally, through the overt mention of the sound of the shoes and the poetic effects of alliteration and sibilance. The half-rhyme on which the poem ends carries an echo of the steel, perhaps like the sound of the newly shod mare stepping on the stone of the farmyard floor.

'The Farrier' is reminiscent of poems of rural work such as those in Seamus Heaney's earliest collections, *Death of a Naturalist* and *Door into the Dark*. Like the subject of Heaney's 'Thatcher', Sheers' farrier seems to have almost preternatural powers. The opening image casts him in a priestly light, since his movements are like 'blessing himself'. The 'smoke slow-turning from his mouth' adds mystery, which is complemented by the 'apparition of smoke' that he causes to rise from the horse's hoof later in the poem. The farrier is presented as being hardy and associated with nature: the wind is personified as 'twisting his sideburns in its fingers' and Sheers clothes him in a 'leather' apron that is the 'black and tan of a rain-beaten bay' (a bay is a brown-coloured horse). As well as being tough, the farrier is gentle. Patiently he awaits the mare in the second stanza, and when he lifts the hoof to commence working on it in the fifth he does so like 'a romantic lead dropping to the lips of his lover'. The metaphor suggests attentiveness, courtliness and grace, and the sense of the horse as a beautiful woman to be served continues in the image of the farrier gripping nails in his teeth like 'a seamstress pinning the dress of the bride'.

In addition to presenting the farrier and his work, the poem also provides a detailed and accurate picture of the horse. Notice how the third stanza privileges the mare's perspective. In keeping with the idea that horses use their sense of smell to greet one another, she 'smells' the farrier, noting 'woodbine, metal and hoof'. The next detail, of the farrier avoiding eye contact, is also significant since staring can be interpreted by horses as threatening behaviour. Sheers is also attentive to the fine details of shoeing and uses specialist equine vocabulary such as 'fetlock' (the part of the leg above and behind the hoof) and 'frog' (the pad in the sole of the hoof).

Sheers' farrier is unnamed. This defines him by his job, and Sheers' use of the definite article ('The') makes him seem more of an archetype than a specific person. His job has been done by men like him for generations, and it is presented with an air of mystery and expertise, which leaves the reader feeling impressed and respectful towards country traditions.

Taking it further ▶

Hear Owen Sheers reading the poem by visiting www.poetryarchive.org and searching for 'The Farrier' in the search box. Click on 'Owen Sheers' and a list of his recordings will be displayed.

TASK

Compare the ways in which Sheers and Heaney present rural life and work. You might choose to comment on some of the following: 'The Equation', 'Late Spring' and 'The Farrier' by Sheers and 'The Harvest Bow', 'Glanmore Sonnet I' and 'Glanmore Sonnet IX'.

'Inheritance'

The speaker reflects on the parts of him – both physical and psychological – that have been inherited from his parents. The poem explores heredity and influence, closeness to the landscape and love.

Commentary Sheers uses a seven-line stanza (a heptet) for each of the first two stanzas. One lists the qualities derived from his father, the other lists those derived from his mother. The poem concludes with a sestet (a six-line stanza) in which he lists attributes inherited from both parents, perhaps implying shared attributes: in addition to passing on individual traits, they have a further influence as part of a couple.

The tone of this autobiographical poem is grateful and affectionate. Even his inherited stammer is treated with acceptance and gives rise to an impressive simile: the 'stammer/like a stick in the spokes of my speech'. As well as being evocative visually and perhaps redolent of fathers, sons and bikes, the subtle use of sound creates a gentle stuttering effect as the 'st' sound from the last word of the first line catches with the 'st' sound of the 'stick' in the second. The same technique mimics the persistence of the sound on which a person might stutter as the 'sp' sound of 'spokes' catches in the 'sp' sound of 'speech'.

The 'tired blink' is mentioned in the next line – the poem's shortest – briefly intruding like the action it evokes. The two following lines that complete the poem's first sentence go closer to the core of the poet's character: the need to be near to nature goes right to his 'bones'. These prominent lines contrast with the previous three – which were of uneven lengths, gentle and conversational – by being visually similar on the page and more insistent. The final three words of each line are stressed and the conviction of the statement is enhanced aurally: the first letter of 'have' and 'bones' on one line alliterate subtly with the first letter of 'hill's' and 'bare' on the next and the near full rhyme with 'bones' and 'stone' provides a couplet-like reinforcement of the idea. The final two lines of this stanza continue the sense of the poet's identification with nature, derived from his father (who worked as a planner) with his paradoxical 'affection for the order of maps/and the chaos of bad weather'.

Recognising the complexity of genetic inheritance and personality continues in the second stanza as the poet turns to his maternal inheritance and acknowledges his 'sensitivity to the pain in the pleasure'. There is a sense of enjoying the outdoors that has been inherited from his mother too, but unlike the elemental closeness from his father and the embracing of the chaos of bad weather, there are, from his mother, 'quiet moments beside a wet horse'. The image is of the poet, perhaps with his mother, in a stable as the rain beats down outside and he listens to the noise of a joiner's lathe nearby. Perhaps there is a sense of literary inheritance through Sheers' mother. Sheers' mother worked as a teacher of English and drama and the 'rain-loud' stable is a poetic compound adjective reminiscent of W. B. Yeats' 'bee-loud' glade in the poem 'The Lake Isle of Innisfree'; the idea of the joiner 'turning fact into fable' might suggest that it was from his mother that he inherited his literary inclinations.

Build critical skills

In a review Sarah Crown wrote: 'In "Inheritance", in which the poet acknowledges his debt to his parents, there is a sense almost of marvel at the beautiful simplicity of their lifelong union. This is reflected in the poem's dialectical structure, in which individual verses on father and mother lead to the joyful synthesis of the final verse' (The *Guardian*, 25 February 2006). How far do you agree with Crown's view of the poem?

The final stanza, which disrupts the pattern by being a sestet, reflects on what the poet has been given by both parents together. Sheers uses the extended metaphor of forging perhaps to suggest that their lives are rooted in the substantial and connected to a traditional and dependable country lifestyle. In this way it relates to 'The Farrier', the poem that precedes it in the collection. Yet Sheers' presentation of 'shared lives' is unsentimental: that things have to be tried and might possibly fail is conveyed by 'testing'; that life involves pain and difficulties is suggested by the 'hard hammer' (which also produces a pleasing echo of the 'stammer' from the first stanza). It is, the poem's subtext suggests, enduring hardships together that strengthen a relationship. While it has a malleable 'red hot centre' like a freshly fired horseshoe, its 'cooled dark' sides show this relationship to be as strong as hardened iron.

This paradoxical thermal image is an appropriate note on which to end. Sufficiently non-specific to represent a range of the virtues of the poet's parents, it underscores the complex and paradoxical nature of the building of a character, an identity or a relationship. It is interesting too that this, the most elaborated image of the poem, conveys not affection for the mannerisms, physical attributes or preferences that have been received by the poet, but 'a desire' to have something that they have worked at. This is something less tangible than blue eyes or a tired blink – something that they have shown by example and something that will depend on the poet's own life rather than be a genetic inheritance.

The poem begins with an epigraph, '*After R. S. Thomas*'. In this case 'after' means in the style of, in imitation of, or in honour of, suggesting not only that the poem is about biological, but also literary, inheritance. The poem to which the epigraph alludes is 'Gifts', published by R. S. Thomas in a collection called *Pieta* in 1966. This poem differs formally from Sheers'. It is divided into two halves: the first is a tercet about the 'gifts' the speaker received from his father and mother, then a single line about what he received from his country; the second is a tercet about the gift he gives to his wife and a single line about the gift that he gives his son.

'Marking Time'

'Marking time' meditates on the mark that has been made on the speaker's lover's back. He recalls the night when lovemaking on the carpeted floor produced the mark, which resembles two flags. Tracing the flags with his fingers, he likens them to the marks that lovers make on trees. Even though it is fading, the scar will always be there.

Commentary This poem starts a sequence of love poems which concludes with 'Keyways'. It is, loosely speaking, a sonnet – a typical form for a love poem – but it has been composed in free verse unlike one of the more metrically regular traditional forms such as the Shakespearean or the Petrarchan sonnet.

Sheers' first stanza, comprising seven lines, begins with an image of 'that mark upon your back'; then the speaker recalls the night during which it was

Taking it further ▶

Study the R. S. Thomas poem 'Gifts' (online at www.rsthomas. blogspot.com). Analyse the similarities and differences between this poem and 'Inheritance'. What do you think each poem has to teach us about identity?

Taking it further ▶

You can find out more about R. S. Thomas and issues surrounding Welshness by reading the article on Thomas by Chris Saunders in *The English Review* (Vol. 20, No. 3, pp. 18–20).

produced. The first line of his second stanza focuses on the 'scar' in the present and its 'disturbance' before returning to the experience that produced it and then likening the scar to the marks made by lovers on trees. Many sonnets conclude with a couplet, and perhaps we might think of the final two lines as a couplet of sorts, or at least as offering the kind of conclusion that a closing couplet in a sonnet often does, as he expands on the implications of lovers' marks and how 'though changed, under the bark, the skin,/the loving scar remains'. The internal half-rhyme (on 'changed' and 'remains') provides an aural link, which sounds a note of conclusion, for many readers emphasising the hopeful message that, even though the scar will fade, at a deeper level it, and their love, will remain.

Context

The sonnet is one of the most enduring poetic forms. The term comes from an Italian word meaning 'little song' and its subject is usually an aspect of love. Shakespeare wrote a sequence of 154 sonnets; we now give the name 'Shakespearean sonnet' (or 'English sonnet') to one comprising three quatrains and a couplet and rhyming *abab cdcd efef gg*. A Petrarchan sonnet has an octave (eight lines) followed by a sestet (six lines) and usually rhymes *abbaabba cdecde*.

Others might detect a tone of dissatisfaction in the final two lines, which, it might be argued, is entirely appropriate to what went before. Rather than reading the poem as a straightforward expression of love that uses the marks as a stimulus, one might say that it juxtaposes images of love and lust with a sense of passion fading through time. For example, while a dominant reading might stress that the images of the night when their 'lust wouldn't wait for bed' – during which vigorous sex and a coarse carpet combined to produce friction burns – are presented as urgent, mutual and exciting, it could be argued that these images are also violent and overpowering. Love is personified an assailant who 'laid us out upon the floor' (to lay someone out in a colloquial sense is to punch them unconscious). An even more developed oppositional reading might suggest that there is a subtext of the male possessing the female. Laying, or 'getting laid' is, after all, a crude, laddish way of referring to sex. In addition, the flags, while primarily representing the shape of the marks, might be read as badges of ownership – a reading that might be further substantiated by the mention of 'brand-burn' (farmers often brand their livestock as a means of identifying the animals as their own).

The relationship is presented ambiguously in the second stanza too. The loving gesture of the speaker tracing his fingers along the small of his lover's back is offset by his feeling 'the disturbance again' and remembering 'the still waters of your skin broken, the *volte* engaging'. The 'volte' in this line is ambiguous. The term means 'turn' and can refer to the sudden movement away from a thrust in fencing, or the sideways circular movement of a horse; it also has an intertextual or self-referential resonance since 'volta' is the term given to the point in a sonnet when there is a definite shift in thought, direction or emotion.

In a Petrarchan sonnet the volta comes after the first eight lines (or octave) when there is a shift in mood or subject matter which carries on through the final six lines (the sestet). Perhaps we might, therefore, consider the poem in this form of eight lines followed by six lines: the present tense experience of the speaker looking at the addressee's marked back followed by the recollection of the experience that scarred her (the octave); then the contemplation of the scar, which develops into the simile of the scar as a lovers' mark on a tree (the sestet). The carvings alluded to in this second part (or sestet) could be interpreted as natural symbols of ongoing mutual love, as is supported by the use of both 'equation' and 'equalled' on the same line. But the 'arrow' that is central in such calculations 'buckles' and the marks will fade.

The scar is also fading 'the way our memory will' and perhaps there is a sense that time will also fade their love. If read in an elegiac tone the poem might be understood as coming from a speaker looking back to the peak of passion but recognising the inevitability of separation. The title of the poem might support this reading since, as well as being the mark of a particular occasion – that night of lust and friction – 'marking time' is also a term for time standing still. Soldiers who mark time march on the spot, and perhaps that is the point that has been reached in the relationship: the couple are no longer progressing, but only going through the motions. The final line highlights that 'the loving scar remains'. The oxymoron is prominent: we are shown a symbol of love, but we must also recognise it as a mark of hurt; that it is 'changed' perhaps shows that time is a healer, but that it 'remains' points to the lasting impact of the pain. Significantly, while the making of the mark was mutual, the only body to remain scarred is the woman's.

> The carvings ... could be interpreted as natural symbols of ongoing mutual love

'Show'

The speaker attends a fashion show with his girlfriend. After an argument, he leaves their hotel room and sits in the bar alone. Later, his girlfriend, attractively dressed and made up, enters. He forgets their former disagreement and is struck by her beauty.

Commentary 'Show' is an interesting title that most obviously denotes the fashion show in the first stanza or a performance in general, but it might also suggest artifice, the idea of things being superficial, or done for show. Ostensibly about love, or even young urban life, the poem might also be about superficiality.

It is divided into two distinct parts indicated by Roman numerals. The first (in three tercets and a two-line stanza) is largely image-driven and evokes the experience of being at a fashion show; the second is more narrative, is written in quatrains (four-line stanzas) and it tells the story of a tiff followed by renewed feelings of love.

This is a poem in which the visual sense acquires a heightened importance, and in which visual pleasure at times almost takes on the proportions of **scopophilia**. While the poem does show a kind of voyeurism, it could be argued that, rather than encouraging the reader to share in voyeuristic pleasure, Sheers is actually highlighting superficiality and pointing to the absurdity of the fashion industry.

The short tercets and the two-line stanza in the first part of the poem are perfect for rendering the fashion show. Each one allows Sheers to hold an image or two for a moment before moving on. The first is reminiscent of a **haiku**; it depicts the models as birds – 'curlews' – and captures the sense of their slimness, long legs and distinctive walk. In one sense it shows them as elegant, in another, ridiculous. The ambiguous portrayal continues in the second stanza, which turns the camera on to the speaker and the spectators who are metaphorically 'at a slow motion tennis match'. At the close of this stanza and the beginning of the next, Sheers captures the characteristic end-of-runway turn and pose, before finishing the first part of the poem by focusing on the fashion industry's insatiable desire for visual stimulation as the 'crocodile pit of cameras' flash 'their teeth for more'.

Sheers turns from the impersonal world of the show to the personal narrative of the speaker and his girlfriend in the second part of the poem. It begins with a sense of separation – 'I leave you' – and concludes with an image of reconciliation. The quatrains, which are a typical stanzaic form for storytelling, seem substantial after the brief tercets and the two-line stanza of the first part, which evoked the superficialities of the fashion world. Yet the influence of the former part remains: his girlfriend is paying attention not to him, but to her reflection. While creativity is implied by the references to art and music, discord is also suggested. The poem has moved from the inclusive 'we' of the first part to the distinct forms of 'I' and 'you' in the second. Perhaps a change in the speaker's attitude to this beautiful woman is suggested subtly by his response to her eyelashes, which he notes have moved from 'fine' to 'bold'. A petty argument might have been the cause of the separation, as could be suggested by the first line of the second quatrain in which the speaker closes the door 'on this scene'.

scopophilia (literally, 'love of viewing') a term used in cinema studies to denote the voyeuristic pleasure derived from gazing – usually at the female form; the male is the active subject and the female the passive object. It could be argued that the poem is subtly criticising this kind of superficial pleasure.

haiku the Japanese form that compresses an image and idea into three lines of five, seven and five syllables respectively.

◄ Models at a fashion show

Whatever its cause, the loss of love does not last, and the poem culminates in a two-quatrain image of reconciliation – or, more precisely, an image of a beautiful, well-groomed woman. Some might see this as a romantic picture of the man seeing his lover anew in a breathtaking image of perfection. It might also be seen in a larger context: as representing the power of women to transform themselves through make-up and adornments – something that has been done since virtually the start of civilisation. This power is certainly presented in the poem. Whatever the nature of the battle that the couple might have had before the narrative began, after her transformation it is clear that the woman has won: she leaves the speaker 'surrendered'. Rather than read the image of the woman and her new look favourably, others might argue that it is an intentional composite of idealised perfection: the kind of perfection that the fashion industry sells; the kind of image that is really just a show.

Sheers also makes ingenious use of rhyme to evoke the move from a sundering to a reunion. There are no rhymes in the first five lines of the second part of the poem, but rhyme gradually strengthens as the couple move together: the second quatrain has a half-rhyme on 'corridor' and 'more', the third a full rhyme with 'skin' and 'in' and the final quatrain uses envelope rhyme – two rhyming lines that enclose other material (in this case a couplet). This has the effect of heightening the impact of the central image by framing the couplet – the image of the beautiful woman – and making it stand out.

Rhyme gradually strengthens as the couple move together

This technique is complemented by the sense of the last line: she looks glossy and sharp, while the rest of the room blurs into insignificance. The term 'out of focus' could have another connotation: it could end this poem of seeing and surfaces by drawing our attention to another visual trick. Despite the impact of her entrance there is no real sense of the woman as a person: there is much attention to her dress and adornments, but little about her character; perhaps the implication is that the speaker has been bewitched by a woman whom he doesn't really know. Trickery is also suggested by 'hocus-pocus', 'spell' and the kind of magic performed by make-up, clothes and jewellery. Such magic, it could be argued, is calculating, superficial and a great deal less substantial than the more wholesome magic that takes place away from the superficiality of the city and is demonstrated by the subjects of poems such as 'The Farrier' and 'The Equation'.

Context

In 1999, Owen Sheers won a young writer's award from the fashion magazine *Vogue*.

'Valentine'

The speaker addresses his girlfriend (the valentine of the title) recalling three memories from their trip to Paris. The first might be an image of a break-up, as the speaker follows his lover down an empty street; the second shows his desire for her as he watches her body, but the 'wet lashes' might indicate tears; the final image is one of reconciliation as they hold each other on the bed of the hotel room. This final memory is the one he will keep.

Commentary This enigmatic poem evokes some of the images, feelings and ambiguities of love. While not, strictly speaking, a narrative poem, its images have been sequenced so as to suggest a story. This story, in the form of three memories, is structured in two parts: the first eight lines being two memories of discord, and the last seven a single memory of the making up. Although 15 lines long, rather than 14, the poem resembles a sonnet in terms of its subject matter and its volta-like shift in tone after the octave-like first part and its final couplet. The first part of the poem also resembles the form of R. S. Thomas' 'Gifts' – the poem that inspired Sheers' 'Inheritance' – with each tercet being followed by a single line that is a complete sentence. That two tercets are used for the memory of reconciliation perhaps implies that this happy memory balances the other, more troubled, two. The sense of a resounding conclusion is provided by the final line, which ends with a full rhyme and addresses the girlfriend directly as 'my valentine', thus linking the poem's subject matter to its title.

Taking it further ▶▶

Find out more about the sonnet form at http://tinyurl.com/24pa3ub or at web.cn.edu/kwheeler/poetry.html.

Context

Poets have always stretched the boundaries of genre. Shakespeare's Sonnet 99 confounds expectations of the form by containing 15 lines, while his sonnet 130 confounds expectations of the genre by seeming to denigrate his mistress, who readers would expect him to praise - before we realise that he is actually satirising the falseness of other sonneteers. Carol Ann Duffy has also written a poem entitled 'Valentine'; hers eventually satisfies readers' expectations by communicating passionate love - but first it confounds them with her bizarre choice of Valentine's gift: an onion.

The title, and indeed the poem's setting, create generic expectations. 'Valentine' might make us expect a straightforward love poem in praise of a loved one; as it is set in Paris, a city synonymous with love and lovers, such expectations are enhanced. But a literary text does not always give pleasure by simply conforming to generic expectations; the reader also gains pleasure when a text confounds these in interesting ways. In Sheers' poem there are no recognisable sights of what many consider the most romantic city of the world; instead there is an empty Paris street as the speaker, possibly after an argument, is following his girlfriend. If the intention was to have a romantic city break on Valentine's day, then things have not gone as planned.

The reader is immediately placed in the middle of the action in the present tense, and, perhaps like the speaker at the time, is not completely sure what is happening. Inanimate objects are used to suggest some of the couple's feelings. The high heels, which are often a symbol of confident female sexuality – they give a woman height as well as elongate her calves, and accentuate her breasts and bottom as she walks – do not arouse, but annoy. The speaker responds to them as 'water torture', and the street down which they walk is 'evacuated as the channels of our hearts'. While this could suggest hearts that have expended much love, it is more likely that it implies their hearts contain no love. The

The reader is immediately placed in the middle of the action

enjambed a line is enjambed when it does not conclude with a punctuation mark.

single-sentence stanza on a single line – 'That will be one memory.' – slows the pace, allowing the reader to contemplate the previous image before the speaker moves on to the second and the pace picks up. The first two lines of the third stanza are **enjambed** and allow the reader to see what the speaker does as he walks after his girlfriend: 'The swing of the tassels on your skirt/each step filling out the curve of your hip'. While these details show an appreciation of the female form, the speaker seems to be an observer: as in the first stanza, there is a disconnection between him and his girlfriend. The final line of this tercet closes on a detail of the girlfriend's 'wet lashes, the loss of everything we'd learnt', which implies that there has been a tearful argument, the result of which has been a break-up and the loss of their relationship.

While the first part of the poem confounds our expectations of a love poem, the second part meets them by providing a familiar image of a couple 'holding each other on the hotel bed' as well as an extended simile that shows a grateful reunion. The simile compares the lovers to 'a pair of wrecked voyagers/who had thought themselves done for': presumably the storms were the tempestuous rows and the shipwreck their temporary break-up. The waking 'washed up on the shore' and the 'exhaustion' might evoke their recovery after the extreme emotions of the split as well as their feelings after having been physically close once more. The paradox in the final lines of the stanza, when they are uncertain 'whether to laugh or weep', evokes the overwrought state of mind produced by their intense relationship and the bittersweet feelings that love can bring. Some readers might be reminded of the characteristic mentioned in 'Inheritance': 'a sensitivity to the pain in the pleasure'. Indeed, the final resounding line of 'Valentine' could be said to exemplify this. There is an elegiac quality that seems to suggest that even in the joy of love there lies a hint of future sorrow. While the memory of the reunited lovers and their passion and tenderness on the hotel bed is what the speaker will 'keep', we should also note that what this final word rhymes with is 'weep'.

'Winter Swans'

The speaker and his girlfriend walk round a lake. They do not speak until they see swans land on the water. They dive together impressively. The speaker's girlfriend tells him swans mate for life. As the couple walk on, the speaker notices that his and his girlfriend's hands are together and that they resemble the wings of a swan.

Commentary 'Winter Swans' is both a love poem and a narrative poem. It comprises six tercets and a two-line stanza, which tell the story of one afternoon in the life of a couple. After two days of heavy rain a dry spell provides an opportunity for the couple to go walking. The narrative proceeds evenly: the first eight lines form a single sentence that describes the walk up to the point when the swans stop the couple by diving in unison.

Despite the romantic elements such as the walk together and being in a place of beauty (we might imagine the walk taking place in the Lake District), in the second stanza there are images that undermine our sense of the couple's love. The earth is 'waterlogged' and 'gulping for breath'; 'gulping' is an ugly-sounding onomatopoeic word that suggests discomfort or embarrassment rather than romantic intimacy, and indeed the couple are said to be 'silent and apart'. Perhaps there has been a cooling in the relationship or some awkwardness rather than a complete break-up; whatever the exact circumstances, so far, the mood of the poem is downbeat.

The swans, however, provide a turning point in the narrative and their aquatic skill and beauty enliven the third and fourth stanzas, contrasting with the previous sense of gloom and dullness. Their arresting 'show' is a composite of ballet, magic and swimming as they perform a synchronised dive, make half of themselves disappear 'in the dark water' and bob up again with aplomb 'like boats righting in rough weather'. Such avian acrobatics seem infinitely more impressive than the absurd performance of the models who were compared to 'curlews' in 'Show'.

Seeing the swans affects the couple. The girlfriend declares that 'They mate for life' – a statement that might be said to put thoughts of both fidelity and sex into the mind of the speaker. While he doesn't reply directly – as elsewhere in the poetry of Sheers – nature moves in mysterious ways: there is a brightening in the weather, which contrasts with the earlier rain and 'waterlogged earth', and he notices that he is holding his girlfriend's hand.

The penultimate stanza transforms the hands of the couple into swans which have 'swum the distance between' them. Any discord in their relationship seems to have been dispelled by these majestic creatures. The final image is given greater prominence by being separated into a two-line stanza of its own – the only such stanza in the poem. The image of the hands like the wings of a swan is both beautiful and resonant. The 'settling after flight' could suggest a contentedness to remain together after a period of separation and the final image of the hands as a swan's 'pair of wings' is one of elegance and togetherness. Taking someone's hand has connotations of marriage and the image of each hand being part of the one pair of perfectly matched wings closes the poem with a wonderful sense of harmony and hope.

'Night Windows'

This is a love poem narrating an occasion when a couple make love in a living room by the light of a single bulb in the hall. They do not realise this makes them visible to those in the houses opposite.

Commentary 'Night Windows' is a painterly poem that is obsessed by the qualities of light and evokes the mood, shades and textures of night-time as well as an appreciation of the female form. It shares its title with a 1928 painting by Edward Hopper, which depicts a dark scene at night. In this painting the only light comes from inside a room at the corner of a building. The viewer's eye is drawn to the partially visible figure of a woman in the room, which is framed by one of the windows. She wears a red slip, which is rising up as she bends down, perhaps to place something on a table out of sight.

While Hopper's painting seems to make the viewer into a voyeur as the eye is led to the woman's body, Sheers' poem makes us identify with the speaker, who is both observing his girlfriend and being watched.

TASK

Compare and contrast the structure and form of 'Winter Swans' with either 'Valentine' or 'Show'. Some areas that you might consider: the narrative and use of time, the stanzaic form and regularity, the use of location in each narrative.

CRITICAL VIEW

The New Princeton Encyclopedia of Poetry and Poetics argues that 'a love poem cannot be simplistically read as a literal, journalistic record of an event or relationship; there is always some fictive shaping of reality for dramatic or psychological ends'. To what extent should we consider the use of 'true stories' in this way?

Edward Hopper's painting *Night Windows*, 1928 ▶

The poem narrates the story using quatrains, moving at a languorous pace in keeping with its sense of savouring a time of physical intimacy. While the first stanza creates atmosphere as the couple strive to create the right mood by turning off most lights and leaving 'the hall bulb bright', the second provides a shift in tone through humour as the speaker, looking back, realises that his soft lighting meant that the lovers were visible not just to themselves but to the neighbours. Yet even the voyeurs outside are affected by the poet's sensibility: they do not simply see a young couple having sex, but experience them as an art form, since they are rendered 'impressionist' by being viewed 'through the thin white drapes'.

The next images, which continue from the second to the third stanza, are from the perspective of the speaker who views the woman's curves as though they are from 'a distant landscape'. This type of conceit which sees a woman's body as the landscape is reminiscent of the work of John Donne, who in 'To his mistress going to bed' referred to his lover as 'my America! My new-found land!/My kingdom'. While Sheers' poem lacks the urgency of Donne's, his speaker seems to be deriving aesthetic pleasure from the woman's body, which in the third stanza is 'slick and valleyed/in the August heat'. Some readers might argue that while the poet is not appropriating the female body in the possessive and colonial manner of Donne — it is 'your pelvis' and 'your body' — he is objectifying the female and making the reader into every bit as much of a voyeur as those who watch from the windows opposite. The image of the landscape blends into one of both strength and bliss, as the woman's back is 'arching like a bow'. Unlike Donne's poem, which one might argue positions the woman as the passive party, Sheers emphasises the interdependence of the couple: the 'invisible tendon' of the woman (which is analogous to the string of the bow) is loaded 'with our meeting'.

The focus shifts after this moment of tension to those who watch. They might be seen as prurient or prudish, since 'Morse codes' suggests that some make flashes by closing their curtains then opening them as they return for another look, while others draw their curtains briskly in disapproval (a 'side-swipe' can be a dismissive and off-hand remark).

The final two stanzas grow more impressionistic as the poet evokes the effects produced by the light from outside. These visual effects are reminiscent of those from a cinematic genre known as *film noir*. Such films usually deal with crime, are set in cities and feature an isolated protagonist; they typically use various lighting effects to produce shadows and darkness, which often create a menacing mood. The 'only light left' sends a 'blue strobe' – a distorting light that disrupts the brain's perception of movement – across the rooftops. Perceived as a kind of 'lightning' by the speaker, such light is, paradoxically, 'both far away yet near'. The reference to lightning contributes to the darker atmosphere at the end of the poem, which, for some readers, might be furthered by its source: a police car or an ambulance. Even the use of the word 'siren' could add to the effect, since this can also connote a dangerous but seductive woman.

> The word 'siren' could ... connote a dangerous but seductive woman

Indeed the woman of the poem might be seen as being presented in the manner of a *femme fatale* (a beautiful but deadly woman, with whom the protagonist of a *film noir* might become embroiled). The use of the tercet after a poem of quatrains adds power to the depiction of the woman in this final stanza. Everything describes this woman and her actions. With a mood of post-coital languor (or with the implication that she is leaving him), she rises from the speaker 'with a sigh'. The dominant figure, she acts while the speaker merely watches. She walks into the light and the poem closes with a stylish, but mysterious, image of the woman as she trails 'the dress' of her 'shadow behind' her.

'Keyways'

'Keyways' explores the end of a romantic relationship. The speaker narrates the story of going to the locksmith's with his ex-girlfriend to have the keys cut that will enable him to enter her flat and remove his belongings. As he waits, he remembers the times when they were a perfect match and reflects on what went wrong.

Commentary A narrative love poem that explores the end of a relationship, 'Keyways' is more meditative and analytical than the preceding love poems. The five-line stanzas with their relatively long lines allow for thoughts and feelings to be developed in some depth.

The poem is divided into three main parts: the couple standing at the locksmith's; reflecting on their early relationship; and wondering when and how things went wrong. There is also a cyclical effect as the whole story is framed by two sentences that marvel at the strangeness of the situation. Throughout, Sheers exploits the metaphorical potential of locks and keys.

Unlike some of his other love poems, which evoke what could be relationships in trouble but where the status of the relationship remains ambiguous, 'Keyways' begins unambiguously: the couple are at the locksmith's as a consequence of having broken up. The opening stanza has a brisk, matter-of-fact tone and the functional details are reinforced by half-rhymes of varying strength: there is a 'set' of keys to be 'cut' so he can 'visit' the 'flat' when she's 'out' to take his things. While there is little overt emotion or self-pity in the stanza, some readers might feel sympathy for the speaker; he is the one, it seems, who is being rejected, the two of them do not appear to be talking and perhaps things aren't even amicable enough for him to remove his things while his girlfriend is there.

Emotion intrudes in the second stanza when the 'hot day' illuminates the uncut keys along the wall. Ironically, he sees them as 'lucky charms'. Then the narrative moves into the past as the speaker focuses on a single 'edentate' (toothless in the sense of being a blank key without any impressions) key as a metaphor for how he felt when they met. It is interesting that he is characterised as the more passive party; it is she who makes the 'impression' – moulds him until their 'keyways would fit'.

The next image could also be regarded as central in the poem, since it represents proof that their 'keyways' fit – that they are 'keyed alike'. Structurally, it is central in the poem, occurring right in the middle, where it continues across two stanzas. Rather than being a sexual meeting of bodies (as we might have expected from the key and keyhole metaphor) it is a meeting of minds and spirits. Taking place in a chapel, the moment of harmony comes when they listen to Handel's sacred oratorio, *Messiah*. Not only do their bodies touch in several places, but their breathing is also 'rising and falling in unison'.

This union in the chapel leads the speaker to the conclusion that 'our combinations matched' and this gives rise to an image of sexual compatibility as their 'tumblers aligned precisely to give and roll perfectly/into the other's empty spaces'. Such speculation leads to an image of post-coital closeness as the speaker holds on to his lover's back and their 'master key fit' gives a feeling of 'coming home'.

Yet there are hints that all was not as perfect as it seemed. The Siamese twins 'sharing one lung' simile, while suggesting harmony and interdependence, might also suggest frailty, and even though they align perfectly, perhaps there is a suggestion of separateness in the way in which the woman was 'facing away'.

The last line of the fifth stanza marks a jarring shift in tone, as two questions are asked in a single line: 'So when did the bolt slip? The blade break in the mouth?' The penultimate stanza attempts to answer those questions. Continuing to use the metaphor of the locks and keys, the speaker tries to 'unpick' events back to the point when things first went wrong. The metaphor becomes aural as well as visual as the reader tantalisingly awaits a 'click, which never came'. This onomatopoeic word has a faint internal rhyme with 'unpick' and takes us back to

Build critical skills

'Keyways' contains possibly the most elaborated metaphor in the entire collection. Note the different ways in which Sheers uses keys and locks in this poem.

Context

Changing the locks is something usually done to increase the security of a home - sometimes to prevent a former partner from gaining access to the property. For example, the American singer-songwriter Lucinda Williams used the title 'Changed the Locks' for a track about a broken relationship (1988).

the first line of the stanza; this backwards look only serves to reinforce the sense of futility – it is 'useless' to search for answers in the past.

There are no recriminations – from the speaker's perspective it was just that 'one of us made a turn that failed to dock' – and the poem ends by underlining the strangeness and significance of the experience in a final two-line stanza that closes with the image of 'changing all the locks'. This is an appropriate ending: the poem began with the thought of keys and opening and now it closes with the thought of 'locks'.

As well as being a poem about the end of love, 'Keyways' also addresses the central theme of the collection as implied by the meaning of the term 'skirrid' in the title: separation. In this way it links not only to the other love poems in the collection, but to those that deal with other separations or moments of transition, such as 'Border Country', the next poem in the collection.

TASK

For his recording for The Poetry Archive, Sheers included only 'Keyways' and 'Marking Time' from this sequence of love poems in *Skirrid Hill*. For what reasons do you think he chose these and not 'Valentine', 'Show' or 'Winter Swans'?

'Border Country'

This poem explores growing up and deals subtextually with rural decline. It is set in a place where the speaker and his boyhood friend used to play. The speaker returns and evokes the childhood world of playing war and sitting in the driver's seats of abandoned cars, but the real subject of the story is his friend. This boy's father, a farmer who had grown depressed, took his own life by shooting himself in a cornfield. This traumatic event has catapulted him into adulthood and left him mentally scarred.

Context

Wales in the late 1990s and early 2000s was a tough place for farmers. As well as disputes within families over the inheritance of farms and lands, there were widespread difficulties in the wake of the BSE epidemic (which reached its peak in 1992 and 1993) and the outbreaks of foot-and-mouth disease in 2001 and 2002. Farmers' incomes declined, and, in June 2001, a BBC Wales report linked three separate suicides by farmers to the additional pressures they faced as a consequence of the diseases.

Commentary 'Border Country' is given prominence by its position: right at the heart of the collection's first half. Dealing with adolescence, the poem tells a story of death and a boy who was forced to make the leap between childhood and adulthood uncomfortably early. Its title refers as much to the border country of adolescence as to the part of Wales in which it is set. It also carries a sense of the boundary that the speaker has crossed – into a stable adulthood beyond rural Wales – but which still constrains his boyhood friend. This poem has possibly the most detailed narrative in the collection, and its unusual nine-line stanzas enable the poet to develop his story in depth as well as to create subtle structural effects.

exposition the opening part of a narrative that introduces the characters and situation.

proleptic foreshadowing; predicting what is to come.

Context

The influential Russian dramatist Anton Chekhov (1860-1904) expressed ideas about raising and meeting audience expectations in a dictum that has become known as 'Chekhov's gun'. It states that if a gun is on the mantelpiece in the first act, it must go off in the third.

The narrative moves in a cinematic manner. The opening image is like an establishing shot. The reader sees the 'car quarry' in the present, before this dissolves into an image from the past and we see the 'elephant's graveyard of cars' where the two boys used to play. Such images have both **expository** and **proleptic** functions. We are made aware of the place in which the speaker and his friend used to play, but there are also elements of foreshadowing. For example, in one image cluster the raised earth resembles 'the hummock of a grave', the trees are like 'a headstone' and the leaves like 'epitaphs'. The tone is elegiac and other aural elements enhance the sense of foreboding: the alliterated 'g' and the half-rhyme with 'gave' lend prominence to 'graveyard' which echoes 'grave', the last word of the end-stopped second line.

The narrative perspective shifts in the second stanza. It moves into the first person plural, and the poem – in the second, third and fourth stanzas – becomes the shared story of two friends. On the surface, the speaker narrates normal childhood experiences, as, for example, the boys play games in abandoned cars and in the open air. Yet even as it evokes a seemingly idyllic childhood friendship, hints of more sinister happenings lurk. Picking up on the grave imagery of the first stanza, Sheers adds further suggestions of death. Words like 'war' and 'dying' are dropped in, and death is foreshadowed by having the boys play with the shotgun in a field. By so doing, Sheers is effectively loading the weapon that will fire at the end of the fourth stanza.

Images and details in the third stanza also prefigure death – 'buzzards' are a type of vulture and might carry connotations of death, and the detail of the boy in the abandoned car 'going nowhere' prefigures his fate at the end of the poem when he is unable to find a direction in life after the suicide of his father.

This suicide is also prefigured subtly through the use of colour and sound. As the boys walk amongst the decaying cars they are:

> reading aloud from the names of the dead:
>
> *Volvo*, *Ford*, *Vauxhall*,
> their primary colours rusting to red.

Any rhyme in a previously unrhymed poem will draw the reader's attention. In this way Sheers links 'dead' and 'red', foreshadowing the event at the end of the fourth stanza when the father shoots himself and his blood stains the field like 'a poppy sown in the unripe corn'. This climactic moment relates not just to the man who killed himself, who was 'unripe' in the sense that he was too young to die, but also to his son, who will be blighted by his father's action. Indeed the whole poem confounds our generic expectations since it is an elegy not so much for the father who died as the son he left behind – who was pitched 'without notice,/through the windscreen' of his youth. The harmless stationary cars have been transformed into a pile-up in a metaphor that builds on the decaying car imagery that has accrued throughout the poem. It also prefigures the story's denouement as the boy has been ejected from safety and is condemned to walk the hedgerows alone.

Sheers gives greater significance to the story by shifts in perspective in the last two stanzas. We move from the first person plural back to the first person singular and the chronology moves forward from the time of the suicide to the recent past. The speaker returns, but the landscape of his childhood has 'diminished' and the magic has gone: there are 'just cars in a quarry'. The visual perspective changes too as the speaker's movements startle a buzzard 'that flew from its branch like a rag'. Reminiscent of the buzzards that flew above the friends' heads in their innocent childhood, this image is sudden and arresting. Some of the trauma of his boyhood friend seems to have been transferred to the bird, which is 'disturbed'. In a detail that might remind some readers of the ending of Alfred Hitchcock's film *The Birds*, the perspective moves upwards as the buzzard spirals into the sky, and the poem closes with the lonely bird's-eye view of the fatherless boy. This broader perspective on which the poem closes helps to give the story a universal relevance. While we may not all have to make the transition from childhood to adulthood so suddenly or so traumatically, we all have to make it in our own way; we all have to inhabit the awkward border country of adolescence.

This difficult terrain of adolescence is also negotiated in poems such as 'Hedge School', 'Late Spring' and 'Joseph Jones'. The abrupt generational shift in 'Border Country' contrasts with the more gentle changes evoked by the two poems that follow it, 'Trees' and 'Farther'. The consequences of death are also central to poems like 'Y Gaer', 'The Hill Fort' and 'The Wake', and, thinking more laterally, it is possible to link 'Border Country' to others concerned with moments of change, rupture or separation. In this way we might compare it to the war poems, or to some of the love poems, such as the one that precedes it, 'Keyways'.

'Farther'

The speaker walks up the hill called the Skirrid with his father and their dog. At the top, the son takes a picture of his father and himself with a view of the mountains in the background.

Commentary This poem and the next, 'Trees', are both autobiographical and deal with the relationship between a father and a son. While personal to the poet they also evoke a wider sense of tradition and affinity with the Welsh landscape. The title is interesting. Phonologically close to 'father', it could also imply moving further away, or it could simply mean progressing. Paradoxically, the poem that begins with the title 'farther' ends with a sense of two people being closer.

Written as a single verse paragraph, 'Farther' has a conversational rhythm and is spoken in the voice of a son recounting to his father a time when they walked together. The poem follows the narrative of that journey, ending when they reach the top of the hill. Laid out as a tall block of text with jagged ends, its physical shape seems appropriate for a climb up a hill. It is set on the day after Boxing Day and might strike a chord with families in which a grown-up son or daughter no longer lives close by, but always visits at Christmas time.

▲ The Skirrid, also known as Skirrid Fawr, near Abergavenny, South Wales

Taking it further ▶

Details of the nineteenth-century interpretation of the legend may be found at http://tinyurl.com/4ohlfup. See also the boxes relating to the final poem in the collection, 'Skirrid Fawr', on pp. 59–60 of this guide.

The first sentence describes the route of the journey and indicates the main theme by an allusion to a local legend – that a 'cleft of earth' was 'split they say by a father's grief'. The grief in question is God's grief at having to give up Jesus, but Sheers foregrounds the human element of the story, making it more relevant to the poem's theme and more resonant with other poems of landscape and fatherhood in the collection such as 'Y Gaer (*The Hill Fort*)' and 'The Hill Fort (*Y Gaer*)'.

The poem conveys a sense of the father having aged as, significantly in the middle of the poem, the pair is 'half way up' when the exertion of the climb has put the father under strain – his head is 'bent' and his breathing 'short and sharp'. The sentence ends with the speaker's thoughts of the 'tipping in the scales of us,/the intersection of our ages': the balance in their relationship has shifted. He recognises that his father is growing older and weaker and will need his strength and support.

The next sentence describes the remainder of the journey to the top, in which a sense of closeness is implied by words such as 'together', 'shared', 'we' and 'us'. There is a sense too of the pair being emblematic of the values that are passed from fathers to sons; they are seen against the backdrop of their country, a love of which they share.

It is not just the heart-warming sense that father and son are close that we feel at the end of the poem, but that they are united by their shared Welsh heritage and identity. This point is reinforced by the poem's only rhyme as the sense of the speaker feeling 'closer to you' takes us back to the sense of them being 'together against the view'.

'Trees'

A father has planted an oak sapling in a field at the family home. He tells the son it will be 'some time' before it is fully grown. The son reflects on this and the previous trees that were planted for each of his father's children.

Commentary Sheers himself refers to 'Trees' as 'a conversation of sorts, I suppose, through poetry, with my own father' (Sheers, 2006, the CD). Like 'Farther', it is another 'tipping in the scales' poem in which a moment of transition in the relationship between a father and son is evoked. The poem comprises six two-line stanzas followed by a single-line stanza, and the experience is divided into two parts: the first six lines recount the conversation and the last seven the poet's reflections.

Conversational in tone and gently paced, the first part of the poem conveys the impression that the father is a softly spoken man of few words, whose nod conveys as much as his speech.

The second part contemplates the significance of what has been said in the first. There is a sense in which the speaker and his siblings have been rooted by their father – and by extension their upbringing – conveyed by the image of the planting of oak trees on their land. Perhaps the points of the compass suggest that the children's upbringing will help them to navigate through life, or that they will always have a place in their family home. A young tree is an image of renewal and growth, and its species, oak, suggests stability and durability and might remind some readers of the proverb 'mighty oaks from little acorns grow', reinforcing the sense of strength and opportunities that the children have gained from their upbringing. The new tree, perhaps taking up a position at the other pole, might offer a sense of completion and be the father's final act of planting on the family's land.

Taking it further

You might like to compare 'Farther' to 'Not Yet My Mother', a poem inspired by a photograph of Sheers' mother when she was 17. It appears in his first collection, *The Blue Book* (2000).

TASK

Compare the ways in which Sheers and Heaney present relationships between fathers and sons. Compare Heaney's 'The Harvest Bow' with at least one poem by Sheers. As well as 'Farther' and 'Trees', relevant Sheers poems include 'Y Gaer' and 'The Hill Fort'.

Taking it further

'Woods and forests' is the title of one of the chapters of *A Poet's Guide to Britain*, Sheers' anthology inspired by the British landscape. This chapter includes a poem by Philip Larkin entitled 'The Trees', which, like Sheers' poem 'Trees', meditates on trees and the ongoing natural cycle of decay and growth. Larkin's poem ends optimistically with 'Last year is dead, they seem to say,/Begin afresh, afresh, afresh.'

What is implied is that the speaker recognises his father's sentiment that when the tree is mature he will be gone. The gesture, then, of planting it is one of looking forward beyond one's own life and wanting to be part of a continuing process of growth and renewal. Perhaps the bow imagery reinforces this, since it might be thought to allude to a time when fathers would help their sons practise shooting with the longbow (there is a medieval law stating that all men over 14 must practise for two hours weekly). The tree bending like a longbow and silhouetted against 'a reddening sky' is a beautiful image combining the sense that what the father has planted represents his demise, his children's future and the natural world of which they are all part.

The 'setting or the rising of a sun' with which the poem ends symbolises both the father's ageing and eventual death (the setting of a sun) and the growing maturity and success of the children (the rising sun). While the whole poem is imbued with respect for the father, this is tempered by the need to look to the future: the last word with the rhyme on 'rising of a sun' reminds us of 'what will become'. (Note also the homophonic pun: 'sun' is exactly the same sound as 'son'.)

'Hedge School'

Ostensibly recounting stories of picking blackberries on the way home from school, the poem expresses feelings about growing up, culminating in an awareness of the potential for violence that exists in boys.

Commentary This poem comprises four free verse stanzas of unequal length. The first, a sestet, sets the scene, describing how the speaker used to pick blackberries every September on the way home from school. Each of the other three recounts an occasion on which blackberries were picked; the experiences become increasingly decadent and dark.

The main theme is growing up and the poem has a sense of the fearful dawning of male adulthood. The title is a pun on 'hedge-school', a place of informal education that flourished in Ireland at a time when schooling for Catholics was suppressed. Instruction would often take place in remote areas, sometimes under the cover of a hedge so that the teacher and students could be shielded from the eyes of passers-by. The implication of the title, then, is that the real education is taking place not in school but outside, and not during lesson time, but on the way home. Organised lessons do not teach the speaker real truths about himself; knowledge about the self is gleaned from experimentation with the natural world.

One of the salient characteristics of this poem is Sheers' use of sensuous imagery. The second stanza describes the blackberries in gustatory as well as visual terms: an unripe red one is 'bitter', just as an older one is 'cobwebbed and dusty'. There is a respect for the fruit, almost a savouring of the connoisseur who can contrast the textures – from the 'tightly packed' hardness of some to the 'rain-bloated looseness' of others – and appreciate one that has matured like 'a Claret/laid down for years in a cellar'.

Build critical skills

Sheers remembers that one of Heston Blumenthal's most repeated phrases as he worked with the cooks in the Fat Duck was 'mouth feel'. How might knowing this, or knowing that Sheers spent time in a three-star Michelin restaurant, affect the way you respond to the presentation of foods and tastes in 'Hedge School'?

The third stanza moves from connoisseurship to gluttony. Adjectives and metaphors are heaped together presenting a rich and cloying picture of over-indulgence: a 'coiled black pearl necklace' becomes 'hedgerow caviar', then the 'bubbles of just poured wine' and lastly – in a finale of sensual overload – 'a sudden symphony'.

A shift occurs in the final stanza and the account takes on a confessional tone when the speaker describes how 'just once' he went off amongst the blackberries not to eat but to destroy. The descriptions lose the precision of those of the earlier stanzas as the speaker's behaviour turns violent; the blackberries are crushed when he closes his 'palm into a fist' and what should have been perceptions of taste become disturbingly tactile: they dissolve 'their mouthfeel' over his 'skin' and his knuckles emerge 'scratched'. His hand is now 'blue-black red', which (as well as sounding like 'blackberried') connotes images of bruises and blood. The final blood images – both the blood of birth ('at lambing') and the blood of death ('as a butcher's') – give rise to the speaker's uncomfortable recognition of 'just how dark he runs inside'.

Context

Sheers' epigraph is taken from *The Pardoner's Prologue*. Chaucer's Pardoner is a bold hypocrite, who preaches powerfully of avarice yet sells fake relics for personal gain. The line used by Sheers quotes the Pardoner talking about those he preaches to: he couldn't care less if their souls go to hell ('goon a-blakeberyed'). *The Pardoner's Tale* is one of wickedness: three riotous young men drink, find a pile of gold and then plot against each other, resulting in their deaths. The epigraph perhaps highlights the potential for evil that exists within boys.

The poem is reminiscent of 'Blackberry-Picking', a famous Heaney poem from *Death of a Naturalist*, which uses blackberrying to show how the joys of childhood turn into the pains of adolescence. Sheers' poem was written as a commission for National Poetry Day, and perhaps some of its rich imagery was inspired by the time that Sheers spent with Heston Blumenthal as poet-in-residence at the Fat Duck in Bray.

'Joseph Jones'

The poem recounts a few exploits from the life of a young man called Joseph Jones who was once well known in his small town.

Commentary This poem begins mid-conversation, as though the speaker is replying to a question that someone else has asked. It takes place in a relaxed context, perhaps at a bar. While the title is a name, the name chosen,

Build critical skills

Jones' exploits in the second stanza seem to relate to what was originally a bikers' initiation rite: if a biker performed a certain sexual act he was said to have won his wings. What are your thoughts about the attitudes to women in this poem, and in what ways are they similar to or different from those elsewhere in the collection?

▲ Marilyn Monroe with skirt 'like an umbrella blown inside out'

Joseph Jones, suggests a type rather than a person: Joseph is a typical Biblical Christian name and Jones is the most common surname in Wales.

The poem offers another slant on the theme of growing up and it makes a good companion piece to the one on the opposite page, 'Hedge School'. While it is easy to laugh at the subject, he is also a figure to be pitied, and Sheers uses the stanzaic form to demonstrate how all the youthful bravado and promise of Joseph Jones simply faded; the final stanza has little substance – just a few words on each line.

The tone is of bar-room reminiscences as the speaker recounts his memories of the local character: 'Of course I remember Joseph' comes the reply that begins the poem. The details that are listed seem chosen to entertain the addressee as well as to give a sense of the person described and we gain a sense of Jones' macho pride in his appearance as he goes out on the pull.

The second stanza recounts a tale of Jones' sexual exploits. The woman in the story seems to have been used by him, not even to satisfy his lust, but to enable him to pass an initiation rite or boast to his friends. The story is brought to life for those listening through a vivid visual metaphor of the woman's skirt resembling 'an umbrella blown inside out' and the significant details of her 'white tights shed to high heels'. This might strike some readers as a debased version of an iconic photograph of Marilyn Monroe.

In the third stanza the image of Jones foregrounds his vanity and machismo, but the final one marks a shift in tone. There is no verb and our sense of Jones fades into a few ungrammatical fragments. The trial once with 'Cardiff Youth' hints at lost promise and is made more resonant by the near rhyme with 'small town myth'. All the bravado and posturing, it seems, amounted to nothing, and some might read an even worse fate for a boy who bragged about girls and picked fights: 'a trial' might suggest a court case following a criminal act.

'Late Spring'

The speaker assists his grandfather as he castrates lambs and docks their tails. Weeks later he reflects on the strange harvest.

Commentary 'Late Spring' completes a sequence of three poems about the troubling nature of early manhood. While it depicts a normal aspect of country life – sheep farmers routinely castrate lambs – there is an uncomfortable subtext that seems to be typical of Sheers' depictions of dawning masculinity. The grandson in the poem derives a sense of male potency by taking potency away from other creatures: it made him 'feel like a man' to 'castrate the early lambs'. The title, too, is resonant since late spring is when the lambing season is coming to an end, and so too is the speaker's childhood. This poem also links to others in the collection that feature rural life such as 'The Farrier', which describes with precision the subject's work, and 'Border Country', in which a depressed farmer commits suicide in his field. There is a sense in these poems of revealing rural life to a wider audience; Sheers' depictions are far from the pastoral images that might crowd into the minds of city dwellers. In Sheers' countryside the blackberries draw blood and the little lambs get castrated.

A lyric poem with a strong narrative, 'Late Spring' uses eight tercets and is structured in three parts. The first stanza introduces the subject matter of the story (castrating lambs); the next five provide details of the process; and the last two reflect on the experience. The use of tercets helps with economy of narration and description; in the second section in particular, it allows each image to linger.

The speaker's first job in assisting his grandfather is to load the tool which will castrate each lamb. The technique is to stretch a rubber band around the base of the lamb's scrotum, then release it so that the band tightens, causing a loss of blood to the scrotum, which shrivels and falls off weeks later.

Some readers might see the object with which he removes the animals' capacity for sex as a **phallic symbol**: 'tool' is sometimes used as a slang term for 'penis'; this one is 'heavy and steel-hard' and it certainly seems a symbol of male power and domination. As the speaker makes it ready, his grandfather holds a lamb 'between his legs/to play it like a cello'. The simile suggests both the man's skill and the passivity and naivety of the lamb that he plays.

This playing involves the grandfather coaxing the lamb's testicles into its scrotum – 'two soaped beans into a delicate purse' – so that it is ready for the band to be applied. Male readers, in particular, might find this tactile and visual metaphor uncomfortable reading. The other actions might also strike some readers as disturbing – the grandfather rubs at the lamb's testicles 'like a man milking'. The thought of a woman hand-milking a cow is a pleasing pastoral image in which milkmaid and animal exist harmoniously; milking a cow is necessary for its well-being and the animal may even derive pleasure from it. What is being done by the man in the poem seems a perversion of such a process: this 'milking' is not for the benefit of the animal and it will produce nothing but pain.

Other images contribute to the sense of the astonishing brutality of male work: after he passes the loaded tool, the grandson can only 'stand and stare' as his grandfather's 'clenched fist' opens to 'crown' the scrotum. The image of the fist is typical of male aggression and readers might remember it from the climactic stanza of 'Hedge School', in which the speaker turned from eating to destruction. The use of the verb 'crown' is ironic: far from being treated like royalty, the crowning act for the lamb is castration.

Context

The Russian critic Viktor Shklovsky uses the term 'defamiliari sation' for the technique of making the ordinary seem strange – forcing readers to perceive everyday objects in unfamiliar ways. Perhaps we might view Sheers' technique like this: he has taken an everyday farming event and presented it in a dramatic and strange way. Think, for example, about the ways in which he describes the tool and his final images of the 'strange harvest'.

phallic symbol a sexualised representation of masculinity (male potency, power or domination), usually an image resembling the penis.

Irony continues in the final stanza as the speaker muses on the experience weeks later having counted the docked tails that litter the field. They lie 'like catkins among/the windfall of our morning's work'. There is a bizarre beauty to the by-products of the male work, but the 'windfall' refers to the recently shed scrotums, which rot like dropped apples on the ground. When the poem concludes with the items being described as 'a strange harvest of the seeds we'd sown' we are presented with a paradox: how can castration be described in terms of fertility?

'The Equation'

The poem evokes the two sides of the speaker's grandfather, who is both a teacher and a farmer.

Commentary After the harshness of the previous poem, this one gently evokes another aspect of the life of the poet's grandfather, who was both a hobby farmer and a headmaster (who taught maths). As well as alluding to the latter profession, the title connotes the way in which he is able to balance two occupations perfectly. The sense of wonder evoked by this poem also provides a balance after the feeling of horror of the previous one. Neither poem tells the whole story about life in the country: the cruel and the magical are both parts of rural life. Sheers uses three quatrains to tell the story, with a single-line stanza at the end to give the final piece of magic more prominence.

The first stanza is formed by a single leisurely sentence that describes the fluent transition from classroom to farm. There is a methodical yet unrushed feel as Sheers describes his subject finishing teaching then 'waving away/the blackboard's hieroglyphics'. His metaphors are both apt and economical: the first carries a sense of waving goodbye as well as erasing, and the 'hieroglyphics' of the second help to set up a contrast with his other life, when he enters 'the sweet methane of the chicken sheds'. It is interesting that in this stanza Sheers presents his grandfather's teaching life through sight, yet his farming life is perceived through smell, perhaps suggesting it is a more 'felt' than 'thought' environment (since smell is the sense that is related most closely to memory and emotion).

The actions of leaving school and tending the chickens are presented as the grandfather's normal routine through Sheers' use of the habitual past tense – describing how 'he'd return'; 'How he'd change'; and how his 'hand would flatten'. Despite the everyday nature of the work, it is presented with a sense of wonder. The way in which chicken feeding is presented also foreshadows the overt mention of magic in the final stanzas as Sheers describes the grandfather's 'leaking fist' and 'a sail of grain unfurling to the birds beneath'. It also contrasts with the image in the previous poem, when the grandfather's fist opened, not to feed, but to castrate.

The poem builds to a climax with the egg that he extracts from beneath the sleeping hen: an action that is simultaneously magic and 'just the way of things'. This conclusion might make us re-evaluate the presentation of work at the start of the poem. Teaching too, in a sense, is shown to be magical, since the grandfather had the knowledge to interpret and explain those enigmatic mathematical symbols, but there seems to be something more colourful and wondrous about the trick that produces 'one egg, warm and bald in his brown palm'. We might compare this to the magic of 'The Farrier', or contrast it to the 'artful hocus-pocus' seen in 'Show'.

'Swallows'

The speaker describes swallows, which are symbolic of the ongoing cycle of life.

Commentary The theme of the poem is the regenerative power of nature, which might remind us of some of the poems of fathers and sons in the collection. For example, in 'Trees' when the father is planting an oak that will outlive him, or in 'The Hill Fort' when the father talks to the son about the permanence of place and the generations that have gone before and those that will come afterwards. There is no individual animal in 'Swallows'; they are always plural and 'there is no seam/between parent and child'.

In a simple form of three quatrains the poem renders avian aerobatics in clusters of images drawn from writing. For example, in the first stanza they are 'italic again' and in the last the metaphor is extended as we see their 'script of descenders'; note how they 'sign their signatures' and how they treat the sky as their 'page'.

We might, therefore, respond on one level to the swallows as writers who entertain and impress, but it is perhaps the less showy central stanza that should command most attention. Rather than simply marvel at their signatures in the sky, we perhaps should recognise their 'flawless' perfection in living through their offspring, which, in a sense, means they are always alive.

'On Going'

The poem is set in a hospital, where an elderly woman has been disconnected from machinery that monitors health. The speaker kisses her cheek and her eyes flicker in recognition before she dies.

Commentary The '*i.m.*' of the epigraph stands for 'in memoriam' (in memory of); Jean Sheers was Owen Sheers' grandmother and this poem is an elegy for her. The gentle and loving tone suits this personal experience, which is structured into two connected parts. The first, comprising two quatrains, is primarily descriptive; it centres on the sick room and the dying woman. The second, also comprising two quatrains, is narrative as well as descriptive; the speaker moves from the distant descriptions of the first two stanzas and enters into the poem, narrating his experience of giving a final kiss to his grandmother, then her reaction and her loss of consciousness.

The opening stanza is intriguing at first. Sheers uses defamiliarisation to make the medical apparatus seem strange. The impersonal nature of the 'instruments' that 'measure, record and monitor' seems at odds with the private, intimate nature of the situation. There is a sense of absurdity in the contemporary drive to

Context

Introducing this poem for The Poetry Archive, Sheers said it was about the swallows that come back every year to his parents' house. He noted that a report on climate change had suggested that swallows could be one of the species we might lose – a prediction he hopes will not come true.

Her being 'ancient' adds a sense of preciousness and delicacy

measure and record, particularly since the machines are trying to take 'the soul's temperature'; how can the ineffable be quantified?

As Sheers begins the last line of the first stanza there is a shift in tone as he turns from the machines to address his grandmother directly: 'But you were disconnected from these'. This implies perhaps that death is inevitable since she has been disconnected from the monitors, but it also might suggest that she is above such considerations: her considerations have gone beyond those of the body and are now those of the soul. In the next stanza she acquires an archetypal quality as she lies like 'an ancient child'. She represents a stage of development that all humans will go through, and the description perhaps suggests that life is cyclical rather than linear: she has not advanced to age and death, but returned to a former state – that of being a child.

Her being 'ancient' adds a sense of preciousness and delicacy to the description, which by the end of the second stanza uses natural imagery to convey her breathing: 'working at the skin of your cheek/like a blustery wind at a blind'. The aural effects provide a gentle sense of the laboured breaths through the hard 'k' consonants and their echoing half-rhymes at 'working', 'cheek' and 'like' as well as through the plosive alliteration on 'blustery' and 'blind'. The blind image might also foreshadow death, since it could remind some readers of the custom of lowering blinds in a house to indicate that someone has died.

The second half of the poem begins with a motif from the first in 'measurement', but here the measurement is emotional not scientific: the speaker, no longer an observer, kisses his grandmother. The preciousness of the first half still resonates as the touch on her 'paper temple' is an act of love. Although the grandmother is dying she is not made to seem passive: she gives the speaker the recognition he 'needed' by opening her eyes before losing consciousness.

Death itself is presented in a gentle, dignified manner. The final two stanzas are a single sentence that proceeds fluently from the speaker's kiss to the 'flicker open' of the eyes and the loss of consciousness when she 'slipped back/into the sleep of their slow-closing'. This final detail might remind us of the blind in the second stanza, and the idea of a blind being lowered to signify death. Aural imagery also enhances the sense of gentleness and dignity: 'sleep' echoes 'slipped'; 'slow-closing' echoes 'understanding' and the use of sibilance, consonance and assonance in the 'sleep of their slow-closing' all contribute to the hushed sense of calm. The long vowels and the soft sounds at the end of the final stanza contrast with the hard consonants at the end of the second, which might help to suggest that the grandmother has moved from a state of discomfort to a state of peace.

The title of this occasional poem also suggests that life is cyclical rather than linear: the subject is his grandmother's 'going', but the term 'ongoing' suggests a continuing process – an idea that is echoed in the 'ancient child' of the second stanza, which might suggest both advanced age and a return to the helplessness of early years. 'Ongoing' also carries the sense that something of the lost one will live on through those who are left behind, and perhaps, by being commemorated in a poem, the loved one's memory will be ongoing, since she will continue to live through the poet's verse.

'Y Gaer (*The Hill Fort*)' and 'The Hill Fort (*Y Gaer*)'

'Y Gaer (*The Hill Fort*)' begins with the speaker considering the hill fort – presumably the Iron Age hill fort to the north of the Skirrid – after he has galloped up it on his horse. As the animal rests after her exertion, the speaker looks out over the land beneath the fort and thinks about the man who lost his son and comes up the hill in foul weather to shout and feel buffeted by the storm.

'The Hill Fort (*Y Gaer*)' tells the story of how the man who lost his son used to bring him up the hill and point out places of interest and tell him about the generations of fathers and sons who have lived there. These shared times together are the reason why he has come to scatter his son's ashes on the hill. The man recognises the power of the hill fort, whose walls not only defend but protect.

Commentary As the titles suggest, 'Y Gaer (*The Hill Fort*)' and 'The Hill Fort (*Y Gaer*)' are two reflections on the same experience; in many ways each poem is a mirror image of the other. Positioned at the heart of the collection, this pair of poems (which addresses a split in a family) marks a split. After these companion poems, most of the others are less personal and many are set in places far from Wales. The use of Welsh words in the title and the use of Welsh landscape give prominence to themes of landscape and heredity, and the poems' subject matter enables Sheers to develop aspects of other important themes, significantly love and loss. The styles of these poems are in many ways typical of the collection, for example, in their use of metaphor and narrative as well as their stanzaic form of tercets. The setting, too, seems typical. The stories of the poems both climax on a hilltop: a place from which things can be viewed from a privileged and wider perspective. In this way we might recall 'Farther' as well as the final poem 'Skirrid Fawr' (which is another name for the Skirrid of the collection's title).

The poems also pose interesting questions about truth. They are based on a true story. As Sheers explains in his introduction to them on his recording for the Poetry Archive, the first poem was inspired by a conversation with a family friend who had lost his 19-year-old son in a car accident and how 'sometimes in a storm he would go up and stand in the hill fort' and it was here where he would 'try and make sense of his grief'. 'Y Gaer (*The Hill Fort*)' was, essentially, an attempt to render that experience poetically. When the bereaved man read the poem he said that even though Sheers had 'kind of got it right', he had only presented one side of the story; Sheers then felt compelled to write another. 'The Hill Fort (*Y Gaer*)' is that other side of the story, which, although on the surface is similar, has actually been written in a significantly different style. We might wish to discuss which poem we prefer, but it is worth remembering that they are not mutually exclusive. One isn't the real experience: each offers a different slant. Each has a different style and each might even address a slightly different audience. Paradoxically, both are true and neither is true.

Although the experience of the grief is mediated by the speaker and not directly expressed by the bereaved man, the two poems could be seen as comprising an elegy, which – as is common in this form – moves from expressed sorrow (at the end of the first poem) towards consolation (in the second). Both poems have a similar structure: in the first two-thirds of each the narrative deals with the main character's experience and the last third with the significance of this experience. Thus, in 'Y Gaer' the speaker rides his horse to the top of the hill fort, then reflects on his understanding of why the bereaved man comes here in his grief.

This first poem is the more self-consciously 'poetic' of the two. Each tercet is elegantly concise and even the title performs a grammatical function as the subject of the sentence in the first stanza. The first line evokes 'a ring', an appropriate image with which to begin a poem that is about encircling in the sense of comforting and protecting, and one that is preoccupied – as indeed is much of the first half of the collection – with the cycle of life. This idea is developed subtly as the illuminating beauty of the gorse around the remains of the fort is described as 'yellow in Winter' and 'diminished come Summer'.

Sheers' narrative moves with a fluent transition from this wide-angle shot of the area around the fort to the closer view of 'the mossy gums/of trench and rampart', suggesting subtly the defensive, protective power of this landscape – an idea that he addresses directly and emphatically at the conclusion of the second poem (thus mirroring and strengthening the previous poem's idea).

By the third stanza we have moved to an even closer vantage point: the 'stone pile' that marks the peak of the hill and the centre of the fort. Our movement up the hill has been swift, like the 'long gallop' the speaker and his horse have just completed, but before we settle to a single perspective, we move closer still: to close-ups of the 'veins mapping' under the horse's skin and the 'smoking embers' of her nostrils. In some ways the poem is typical of Sheers' style. Elsewhere he used similarly dramatic visual techniques. For example, in 'Mametz Wood' he moved fluidly from the wider view of the soldiers 'mid dance-macabre' to the bizarre and disturbing close-ups of their 'absent tongues'. In each case the narrative unfolds cinematically, but this is done unobtrusively, in contrast to the poems in which the use of cinematic language adds a stylised, self-consciously artificial feel. This can be seen in 'Show' when the impact of the well-groomed woman causes the room to go 'out of focus', or at the beginning of 'Four Movements in the Scale of Two' when the speaker, like a film director, orders: 'Cut to us, an overhead shot'.

Build critical skills

Sheers has written that in 'Y Gaer' the fort 'is a place where a bereaved father can vent his anger. Like the ancient fort his defences are down' (Sheers, 2008, p. 32). In what ways do you think this is reflected in the poem?

The images in 'Y Gaer (*The Hill Fort*)' are also reminiscent of others in the collection. The 'veins mapping' might remind us of the poet's father and his 'affection for the order of maps' as well as the 'quiet moments beside a wet horse' that he associates with his mother, in 'Inheritance'. The details of the horse themselves might remind us of 'The Farrier' and its reverence for traditional country lore. All these details seem appropriate to a pair of poems in which the consolations for grief are exposure to the natural world and a sense that one is part of an ongoing family of people rather than simply an individual — sentiments that are evoked in poems such as 'Farther', 'Trees' and 'Swallows'.

The perspective shifts — as it does for many who climb hills — and now that he has reached the top, the speaker gains a sense of the clarity and vision that is possible from this vantage point: the land offers 'an answer to any question'. This idea is echoed in the collection's final poem, 'Skirrid Fawr', when the speaker says that he is drawn back to the hill 'for the answers/ to every question I have never known'. Sheers has also conveyed the power of the landscape in his non-fiction. For example, in an article entitled 'Poetry and place: some personal reflections', he writes that looking from a hilltop both 'makes you think and feel, but also, crucially, makes you think and feel *differently*, from a perspective at once more intimate and more objective' (Sheers, 2008). With this in mind, perhaps we feel that the speaker has now achieved both enough distance and enough empathy to gain an insight into the bereaved man's actions.

There is a sense of empathy between the speaker and the man going out in the storm, and we might recall that the speaker in 'Inheritance' felt affection for the 'chaos of bad weather' and a need to be 'near the hill's bare stone'. The poem reaches an elemental climax as hillside weather provides both comfort and mortification: the wind provides a 'shoulder' on which the man can 'lean full tilt'; he can 'take the rain's beating' and the 'hail's pepper-shot'. It also offers catharsis — or even a kind of primal scream — as he is able to express what presumably he would be unable to in a social context and 'shout into the storm'. He reaches an answer of sorts in the last line when he finds, in the elements, 'something huge enough to blame'. While this is not a completely satisfying conclusion (as might be suggested by the faint half-rhyme between 'storm' and 'blame'), we might feel that by blaming the external world, he is blaming everything and perhaps by doing so is recognising his bereavement as — to borrow a phrase from 'The Equation' — 'just the way of things'.

Balance is a key feature of Sheers' depiction of nature and 'The Hill Fort (*Y Gaer*)' balances the earlier harshness with a softer perspective on the same experience. It is a looser poem, with a more immediately accessible narrative, which seems appropriate to its genesis; it was written to give voice to the man's experiences of climbing to the hill fort 'when he's feeling very positive about his son, when he wants to remember him a very good way' (Sheers, 2006).

The images in 'Y Gaer (*The Hill Fort*)' are reminiscent of others in the collection

Build critical skills

In 'The Hill Fort (*Y Gaer*)' the fort is 'positioned as a place of protection as well as defence' (Sheers, 2008, p. 32). Think of examples from the poem of ways in which it protects and defends. In what ways does this contrast with the way the fort is presented in its companion poem?

The galloping and threatening mare with the nostrils of 'smoking embers' of the first poem is replaced by the gentler depiction of the 'long-maned ponies' that 'graze' on the hillside. The sense of pain and grief as constants in the man's life (evoked by the first poem's use of the habitual present tense) has been replaced by the use of the habitual past to evoke memories of the frequent good times. Despite male reserve preventing the father from actually saying what he feels to his son, the reader gains a clear understanding of 'what he meant' as he pointed to 'all the places lived in/by the fathers and sons before them'. The final stanzas state overtly what earlier poems have implied about heredity and the lasting importance of landscape and community compared to the fleeting significance of individual lives.

While some might criticise the poem as sentimental, we might argue that this is unfair since it could be aiming to achieve an accessible expression of tenderness. Rather than trying to please critics or reviewers, 'The Hill Fort' needs to keep faith with its private primary audience by giving expression to the feelings of a bereaved man. The lines in direct speech are interesting: there is little dialogue in *Skirrid Hill*, but these eight lines seem to capture real speech. The statement that 'from here in this view, 9, 19 or 90 years/are much the same' sounds like something the bereaved man could have said. Indeed perhaps it is better that the mirror image of 'Y Gaer *(The Hill Fort)*' is not expressed in the same compact poetic voice; perhaps having a less mediated version of the experience offers a better alternative account.

Build critical skills

Why does Sheers switch languages the way he does in the titles of the poems? (One has English first and Welsh second, the other has Welsh first and English second.)

Context

There is a sense of the importance of the Welsh landscape in 'The Hill Fort(*Y Gaer*)'. The landscape appears to have a spiritual dimension: with the perspective that an inspiring landscape can bring there is also the comfort that while individuals may die and be replaced by their descendants, this process is entirely natural (unlike in the stranger American landscape of 'Under the Superstition Mountains'). In 'Trees' and 'Farther', the transition between generations (in the context of nature) seems smooth and accepted.

The final two stanzas of 'The Hill Fort (*Y Gaer*)' speculate on the wider significance of the experience, and while much is left for the reader to discover in 'Y Gaer *(The Hill Fort)*', here it is revealed plainly. The pair of poems that began with an image of a ring and defences concludes fittingly with these elements. The penultimate stanza acknowledges the scattering of the ashes from the fort as means of making 'the circle complete', but not just this. There is a powerful sense of the landscape as defender and protector. Just as the wind in the first poem was a shoulder for the bereaved man to lean on, in the second the walls of the castle 'hold him', and the poem closes with an image that takes us back to the previous poem's first line, but this time with a new resonance: of walls which 'protect as much as they defend'.

'Intermission'

A power cut plunges a house into darkness. The speaker and his friend drink and talk by candlelight. The friend remarks that all he wants to do is live long enough to play the oboe and the speaker reflects that it is the 'small victories that matter'.

Commentary The title of this poem relates to a time when a power cut enforced a temporary break in normal life; it also suggests a sort of intermission in the collection. We have just emerged from the largely personal first half of the book, which climaxed with the companion poems 'Y Gaer (*The Hill Fort*)' and 'The Hill Fort (*Y Gaer*)'. After the intensity of those poems of landscape and loss, it seems appropriate that there is a gentler, more heart-warming poem before the second half commences. This sense of the title evoking a break in the middle of a performance is also appropriate when we remember that the collection began with a prefatory poem that used the language of the theatre, 'Last Act'.

'Intermission' begins by using the same narrative technique as poems such as 'Y Gaer (*The Hill Fort*)' and 'Border Country': it opens with broad exterior descriptions before narrowing to focus on people. The first stanza conveys the force of nature as the wind fells 'a chestnut tree', which hits the power lines and plunges the house into darkness. Some readers might read this as Sheers personifying nature as an angry god who is passing a critical judgement on the speed of contemporary life.

On first reading the poem might seem elegiac or to prefigure a time of sadness, since the imagery of the house seems Gothic: there are 'wells of darkness' and 'mine shafts of night' as well as 'flames', 'dust' and 'the world lessened'. But, upon closer inspection, the changes brought about by the power cut are beneficial. The place is still and the mood intimate: the two are 'tipping heels of whisky' by the light of the fire. Rather than the lack of power being limiting, it is liberating. The whisky suggests quiet celebration: they are kicking up their heels, unfettered by computers, phones and other trappings of modern life; they are able to concentrate on the more simple pleasures of drink and conversation.

The comment about the oboe sounds absurd – an amusing bit of banter – but it also speaks of a more important observation that it is these things – the simple pleasures that seem ancillary to our working lives – that do not just matter but 'are in the end, enough'.

'Calendar'

Sheers evokes a separate season in each of the poem's four stanzas. Each has a single image and encapsulates a sense of its given season. The reader is presented with images of swallows on telephone wires for spring, bees in foxgloves for summer, a spider's web between branches for autumn and crows' nests for winter.

Context

The dedication '*For L.*' is for Louis de Bernières, the author of *Captain Corelli's Mandolin*. Owen Sheers stayed with him for an idyllic month while he was playing Wilfred Owen in the play *Not About Heroes*, which de Bernières was producing.

Context

Haiku (also known as hokku, which is Japanese for opening part) were originally composed as introductions to linked poems which were popular in Japan in the thirteenth and fourteenth centuries. Many contain a turn - like a volta in a sonnet - which marks a shift in thought, often indicated by a punctuation mark such as a dash. Each part should be able to stand alone, and each should enrich the reader's appreciation of the other part. For further details of this form see *The New Princeton Encyclopedia of Poetry and Poetics* (ed. Preminger and Brogan, 1993, pp. 493, 1034-35).

TASK

Identify and comment on the ways in which Sheers' 'Calendar' conforms to the conventions of the haiku form. Consider the contents of the Context box as well as the commentary on the poem before you answer.

crotchet a sound with the duration of one beat.

minim a sound with the duration of two beats (two crotchets). Notice the way in which Sheers uses these nouns as verbs.

yonic symbol a sexualised representation of femininity and reproductive power, usually through an image reminiscent of the vagina.

Commentary Each stanza in 'Calendar' is a haiku — a poem written in the traditional Japanese three-line form, which usually evokes an image from the natural world in lines of five, seven and five syllables respectively. Haiku (the noun is the same in both singular and plural forms) usually create a calm mood that allows the reader to meditate on a vivid central image, rendered purely and uncluttered by ideas. The most celebrated writer of haiku was Matsuo Basho (1644–94); his haiku often contain a 'kigo' — a word or phrase relating to the season during which the poem is set.

It is interesting to note the ways Sheers uses sensuous imagery in this haiku sequence. 'Spring' renders the season in terms of sound, giving a sense of the swallows providing the electrical energy required after the dead of winter to recharge us into this warmer season as they '**crotchet**', '**minim**' and 'sing volts down the line'. Sibilance and the image of the bees might evoke a buzzing sound in the haiku named 'Summer'. A tactile sense is also conveyed by the 'nervous' movement implied by the 'lover's first time' and the sense of the bees descending delicately between the 'lips' of the flower. This haiku follows the traditional model by containing a turn, which occurs at the comma in the second line: the second part seems to enhance the sexual symbolism of the first part — the phallic bees penetrating the **yonic** flowers — and the first part — with its pretty flowers and bees — makes the loss of virginity in the second seem both beautiful and natural.

The images for the colder seasons are appropriately less attractive: the spider's web for autumn and the 'nests' in winter. The final haiku might remind us of the medical imagery in 'The Wake', in which X-ray images of lungs showed 'squalls and depressions' on 'two pale oceans'; here the image of the diseased body uses birds' nests in branches as clots 'in the veins'. The final image is ambiguous: while some might view it as disturbing and threatening, others may see a hint of hope. The illness is, after all, only a 'passing infection' and just as spring follows winter, sickness will give way to health.

'Flag'

The poem describes various situations in which the Welsh flag might be seen, then reflects on aspects of Welsh identity and nationalism today.

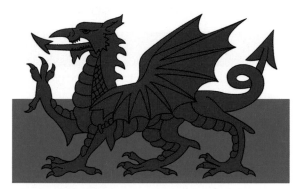

▲ The Welsh flag

Commentary The poem is written in tercets and has a bipartite structure. The first part comprises the first four stanzas. It narrates a journey through Wales during which three separate images of the Welsh flag are seen. The second part comprises the last four stanzas. It reflects on the implications of what has been observed in the first part.

Before both parts comes an epigraph from Christopher Logue's poem 'Professor Tucholsky's Facts', which might offer clues to Sheers' stance on identity and patriotism. In Logue's satirical poem there is something absurd about a person's 'vital organs' being made up of not only internal biological necessities but also 'a flag' – something that is external and socially constructed. In the part that comes directly after this quotation, Logue's speaker becomes progressively more absurd, arguing that while not all of the liver and none of the brain are essential for a man's survival, it is 'impossible' to conceive of it without a flag.

Sheers, therefore, is exploring the centrality of national identity, but also, perhaps, alerting the reader to the absurdity of this seemingly basic human need. Unlike Logue's satirical treatment of national identity, there is a wistfulness and a sense of pathos in Sheers' poem; 'our flag' seems to have acquired a lowly status. Indeed the title of the poem simultaneously suggests both a national banner and a state of weakening. The 'sightings' that the speaker invites the reader to view do not so much show flags of national pride, but show national pride flagging.

The second stanza sees the flag 'strung up on bunting,/hung like wet washing in back yards'. Not only is it presented as being debased by the disparaging comparison to washing hung out to dry, the rhyme also draws attention to its lifelessness since both 'hung' and 'strung up' remind us of a hanged person. If national pride seems dead in the second stanza, in the third it seems worse – it is presented as the faint spirit of something after death. Here, painted on

Context

Issues of Welsh identity and nationalism became more pressing at the time of the referendum on devolution; in September 1997, the Welsh voted, by 50.3 per cent to 49.7 per cent, for a separate legislative assembly for Wales. 'Flag' was written by Sheers after he had been away from Wales for many years and was struck by the number of flags that he saw being flown.

the wall of a gym in Swansea, its form has 'ghosted' to the faintness of 'a bad photocopy'. The final images at the climax of the first part of the poem (which is also the middle of the whole poem) are no more hopeful; they are images of constriction or terminal decline. Here the flag is 'tied to' a snack seller's caravan next to the motorway, 'throwing fits on its pole' and 'struggling to exist'.

Context

The poem's epigraph, however satirical, might spark serious thoughts about the importance of culture. A human was once considered to be composed of layers, with the biological - the body with its vital organs - at the core. The psychological, social and cultural aspects were seen as progressively less important outer layers. The anthropologist Clifford Geertz, however, argues that 'culture … is not just an ornament of human existence but … an essential condition for it' (*The Interpretation of Cultures*, 1973).

Having provided the reader with meagre images of nationalism in the first part of the poem, Sheers looks at its significance in the second part. There is a shift in tone as the language grows more discursive. First he considers the detail of the flag and its dragon, which symbolises Wales. The Welsh word for dragon is *draig*, which means 'warrior' or 'leader', and the dragon might be seen as the proud banner that Welsh warriors traditionally bore into battle. Yet there is little heroism in Sheers' version: the 'facts' can't match the legend and the account of contemporary Wales grows sarcastic as the speaker characterises the nation as 'an old country pulsing to be young'. Like an old uncle at a family wedding who tries to dance and talk like the teenagers, this Wales seems embarrassingly lacking in self-awareness. This lack is widened by the next metaphor, since the country is 'blessed with a blind spot bigger than itself'. A blind spot is usually a small area where one's view is obstructed, yet here it is disproportionately huge.

TASK

If we believe, as Geertz argues, that culture is of central importance and that we require culture to function as human beings, how might that shape our response to 'Flag' and other Sheers poems that address national identity?

Sheers continues by contemplating the flag itself once more and bringing back the motif of the journey westward from the first stanza. Organic images portray it 'spawning itself' and being a 'strange flower that flourishes best/in the barest of places'. Despite their sense of growth, these images – like the epileptic flag of the first part which was 'throwing fits' on its pole – carry a disturbing subtext as the poem reaches its conclusive image. The poem's final flag is the only one that some readers might view as being sited in a fitting place, 'above a town hall'. However, the image is not a departure from, but a continuation of, what went before. The flag is 'wrapped up in itself'. One meaning of this idiom is a lack of self-awareness. The other, more literal, meaning gives rise to the diseased and disturbing imagery of the bandage in the poem's final stanza. (The winding of the flag around the pole in the wind has bound the colours together so that they resemble a 'Chinese burn of red white and green'.)

This concise depiction of the twisted flag that includes both its colours and image of the dragon (evoked by 'Chinese') suggests that Wales is tortured by its inability to live up to the promise of its past. Sheers devotes his final tercet to this image and its significance. As well as being a source of torture the flag, paradoxically, is the 'tourniquet' or the 'bandage' that mitigates the effects of the 'wound' and keeps in check 'the dreams of what might have been'. Not only does Sheers bind several ideas through his image, he also performs a similar feat through rhyme, since an internal half-rhyme binds 'green' to 'dreams' and an envelope rhyme binds 'red white and green' to 'what might have been'. The half-rhyme sounds a note of disappointment, since it emphasises 'what might have been', and the envelope rhyme frames the sense of the flag as a bandage and finishes the poem with a resounding sense of failed promise. Some readers, however, might argue that the poem's conclusion also suggests hope. The flag, like a bandage, has the potential to heal, and the dreams that it prevents might only be fantasies of wishful thinking. Perhaps a new sense of Welshness, with unfurling the flag in more dignified places, might lead to a more realistic direction for Welsh society and a stronger, more healthy Welsh identity.

'The Steelworks,'

The poem begins by describing a deserted steelworks, then turns to work of another sort that goes on elsewhere – men lifting weights. The closing image is of a bleak, grey sky seen through the window of the gym.

Commentary Sheers adds a comma to the title and uses it as a first line; the line that follows wrong-foots the reader, punning darkly on the 'steelworks', noting bluntly that 'it doesn't anymore'. The full stop that end-stops the line adds finality and establishes a gruff mood of discontent.

A shift in tone occurs as the speaker develops rather surreal images, mixing sci-fi with the urban and the pastoral as the steelworks is imagined as 'a deserted mothership' and we see 'sheep passing through the car park' and 'birds nesting in the breathless vents'.

The third part of the poem is set in a gym. Perhaps this is where the unemployed former steelworkers go to pass their time. Connections are implied between the two types of activity: 'pumping iron' reminds us of the work with metal that would have gone on in the steelworks and some of the verbs carry a hint of the work that might have gone on when the men were gainfully employed – they might, for example, have been 'pressing and dipping' in 'lifting bays' of another sort. The sounds and sights of the gym might also be reminiscent of the environment at the steelworks: there are 'pneumatic sighs' and 'strip lights'. Even the term chosen for the time spent at the gym recalls a period spent at work – an 'afternoon shift'.

▲ Ebbw Vale, Wales. Welsh steelworker makes his way home from the British Steelworks of Ebbw Vale

CRITICAL VIEW

'Sheers' depictions of Wales are overwhelmingly dismal and depressing.'
To what extent do you agree with this view? Include some discussion of 'Flag' and 'The Steelworks,' in your response.

Taking it further ▷

For more information on the history of Ebbw Vale, including the closure of the steelworks (and of the coal mines in 1989), go to http://tinyurl.com/3vbuc5w.

Context

The footnote '*Ebbw Vale, 2002*' implies that the poem was written in response to a real event: the closure of steel production on 5 July 2002, which left many in the town without jobs or hope.

The evocation of the gym is purely descriptive: Sheers offers no direct comment on the men's lives and there is no interaction between them. Perhaps they are simply approaching their weight training in the same manner that they once approached their jobs. Alternatively, Sheers might be suggesting that their lives now are empty and purposeless without paid work. For some, perhaps, the gym is a place of meditation or refuge, a secular church in which they kneel, bow and find 'benediction'. For others, it seems to offer an opportunity to spend time, but it provides little comfort: the men 'take the strain' with 'screwed tight eyes' and emit 'pneumatic sighs'. This, I feel, is the over-riding mood, and it is reinforced both by internal rhyme and a half-rhyme with the poem's final word, 'sky'.

The final stanza unites the poem's main elements of imagery as we look through the window of the gym and view a bleak skyscape. The use of 'brushed-metal' for the colour of the sky and the rain falling in 'sheets' are reminders of the materials used in the steelworks; the outlook for the former workers seems to be either unsettled or bleak.

'Song'

The speaker addresses his loved one directly, recounting the actions he would take if they were magpies and she had been ensnared in a trap. Patiently, he would use his wings to protect her from the elements; he would watch the other male birds who would be lured to their deaths by her; he would feed her and sing to her; and, eventually, when the farmer released her, he would be ready to help her to fly.

▲ Two for joy – a pair of magpies

Commentary After two rather pessimistic poems about Welsh identity, Sheers lifts the mood of the collection with two more upbeat poems about love. As the poem's title suggests, this has been written in the form of a song, which – even if it is not set to music and actually sung – may be considered as a poem that is musical in sound and emotionally expressive. 'Song', with its tale of patient love and joyous reunion, certainly fulfils the latter criterion. The poem narrates a story, and the lack of specific detail about the speaker and his lover lend it a fitting, and ballad-like, universality. Of course, 'song' might also refer to the siren-like song of the trapped magpie, which draws the male birds to their death.

Sheers' tercets perhaps allow for the story to be narrated with greater economy and with a greater weight on each image than would be the case in a conventional ballad written in quatrains. The story is structured in three parts. The first two stanzas establish the situation of the poem: if the loved one were to be caught, the speaker would stay with and protect her. The next three stanzas describe how the speaker would watch as the other male magpies were lured by her song and her beauty. The final two form a climax in which the speaker is rewarded for his patience and fidelity when the farmer realises that 'love is all there is to save' and releases his captive. The longer final stanza allows Sheers to emphasise the happy ending. In this quatrain there is also a subtle use of alliteration and a profusion of 'w' sounds that mimic the sense of the wings being tried out once more. The twin notions of flight and release come together in an optimistic finish that ends the poem with a sense of freedom and the implication that faithful, patient love will be rewarded.

For further discussion of this poem see the sample essay of Student D on page 89 of this guide.

'Landmark'

The poem begins at a post-coital moment near a tree, then describes the couple reclaiming their clothes and walking off through the countryside, before stopping to look back at the place where they made love. A landmark has been left, where their bodies have pressed into the long grass.

Commentary The poem makes a rather unusual use of the third person plural, rendering moments of closeness between two people from a distant perspective, almost as if an unseen observer is recounting their actions.

Beginning in the moments after sex, the first stanza depicts the couple as being 'timeless': the intensity of the experience has meant that all else has faded. They have lived in the moment, and this feeling lasts 'for a while' before they must dress and become part of the world once more. By making love al fresco the couple seem to have been at one with nature – the branches of the blackthorn tree act as hangers for their clothes.

In the second stanza, the sense of the lovers being apart from the cares of the world fades as they don clothes and become 'part of things again'. Worldly concerns, symbolised by the 'telephone wires' and 'the time' become central at

TASK
Consider the ways in which Sheers uses birds in the collection. As well as the magpies of this poem there are, for example, swallows in 'Calendar' and 'Swallows' and buzzards in 'Border Country'. Other birds that feature include curlews, swans and chickens.

Taking it further

Many poets have written songs, and some of these function equally well when read, recited or sung. Robert Burns' 'My luve is like a red red rose' is a good example, as is 'Ae Fond Kiss', a set poem in the pre-1900 selection of the AQA *Anthology: love poetry through the ages*. You can hear readings and sung performances of these poems at http://tinyurl.com/dkwsqy and www.bbc.co.uk/arts/robertburns/works/ae_fond_kiss.

the poem's midpoint (in the third stanza) and even nature takes on postlapsarian connotations as they notice 'the broken rug of a long-dead sheep'.

The climax of the poem is when the lovers look back. Here the sense of time is antithetical to what it was at the beginning. Rather than the couple being united beyond time in the intensity of a private moment, it might be argued that they are on the brink of a break-up; their embrace has taken on a sense of desperation 'as if to let go would mean forever'.

The poem's final image adds a cyclical effect by depicting the landmark of the title. What might have been presented as a beautiful natural image of their love together takes on gloomier connotations: the flattened grass where they lay is a 'double shadow' and like a 'sarcophagus'. No longer at the centre of things, the landmark is 'complete without them'. The title itself now seems ironic: we usually think of a landmark as being easily recognisable, important and permanent, but this one seems hidden, inconsequential and ephemeral.

Perhaps we might conclude that the love depicted in the poem is also fleeting. The mournful tone of the last three stanzas might support such a reading. Yet some might argue that the poem does present love's intensity, and that 'holding each other as if to let go would mean forever' emphasises the power of the embrace and the desire for the couple to remain together, rather than foreshadowing a future parting.

'Happy Accidents'

The poem recounts the story of the photographs of the D-day landings taken by the war photographer, Robert Capa, which were damaged during the process of development. Rather than ruining the images, the accidental damage contributed to their impact, somehow adding to the sense of confusion that they depict.

Commentary Like its subject matter, the poem is fast-moving as image tumbles into image. The question in the first line – 'And Robert Capa, how was he to know?' – arouses curiosity. The rest of the poem narrates the events of the photographer travelling with the marines to battle and of his photographs. Narrative events are recounted economically through images: first of the D-day landings, then the act of shooting the film, then others from the darkroom as the film is developed and then images from the photographs, before finishing with images that are simultaneously the photographs and the scenes from the landings that they depict.

The danger and confusion of the war photographer accompanying soldiers into battle are conveyed not only by the images and the pun as Capa hastily has to 'just shoot and shoot', but also by the imagery of the developing process, which recalls bombing and battle. The negative strips 'overheat', 'blister the silver' and 'melt' so that 'frozen fires caught/and smoked'.

Photographic and battle images fuse in the final two stanzas. It is clear that the 'happy accidents' of the title are the mistakes that, rather than ruining the images, help them to 'describe so perfectly/the confusion of that day'. Aptly, Sheers ends this exciting poem on a cliff-hanger of a metaphor – as the soldiers

Context

The title 'Happy Accidents' might remind some readers of the term 'serendipity', which was coined by the writer Horace Walpole in 1754. The term came from the title of a fairy tale, *The Three Princes of Serendip*, in which the heroes 'were always making discoveries, by accidents and sagacity, of things they were not in quest of'.

Taking it further ▶

Aperture Magazine recounts the story of Capa's damaged film. See this, plus further details on Capa and images of his D-Day photographs at http://tinyurl.com/ltetan.

are poised 'to fall headlong through the trapdoor of war'. As in other poems such as 'Border Country' and 'Mametz Wood', Sheers uses half-rhyme to provide a resounding finish, with more than a hint of discontent.

Context

Led by Dr Chenjerai 'Hitler' Hunzvi, the Zimbabwe National Liberation War Veterans Association became feared for its militant tactics. In 1997 it extracted generous payments from the government; in 2000 Hunzvi led the occupation of white-owned farms. Hunzvi was charged with the embezzlement of 45 million Zimbabwean dollars from the War Veterans' funds in 1999; in 2000 he was named as a torturer by Amnesty International. He died in 2001 of an AIDS-related illness.

'Drinking with Hitler'

Dr 'Hitler' Hunzvi is described as he stands at the bar, then turns to talk to the speaker. As he does so, the speaker reflects on the violence for which Hunzvi is responsible. Hunzvi turns his attention to a businesswoman at the bar and flirts with her before leaving with his driver. The woman brushes off his attentions and goes back to her drink.

Commentary The poem presents a vignette of a meeting with Dr Chenjerai 'Hitler' Hunzvi, the late leader of the 'War Veterans', a militant pressure group in Zimbabwe. Quatrains allow Sheers to narrate this story with greater scope than the image-driven tercets that he usually favours. The first evokes a nervy atmosphere as women respond to Hunzvi, a powerful but dangerous man: their 'unsure eyes' are 'switching in their heads'. There is a false, forced quality as the women 'try out their smiles' which are 'brief as fireworks on the night'. Despite his power there is a sense that Hunzvi, like the more parochial alpha male Joseph Jones, is being portrayed as an embarrassing figure, whose own high opinion of himself is unmatched by those of others. Hunzvi 'wears his power like an aftershave,/so thick the women about him flounder in it'.

His own smile is as insincere as those of the women with whom he flirts, but Sheers' metaphor of it coming to his lips like a CD after 'play' has been pressed makes it seem more deliberate, practised and smooth. This smooth image is juxtaposed with the harsh ones that arise in the speaker's mind of the violence for which Hunzvi is responsible. There is a cumulative effect as we hear of 'burned workers' homes', cradled 'bruises' and the beatings that are meted out to the 'first two hundred' when the intended target is nowhere to be found.

There is a shift in the middle of the poem as, after the violent details of the third stanza, the fourth narrates Hunzvi's interest moving from the speaker to the attractive Zambian businesswoman. Like the fictional Joseph Jones, Chenjerai Hunzvi commands attention as he stands at the bar. He conducts 'asked-for laughter', but we suspect that such laughter is more a product of fear than mirth.

TASK

'Mametz Wood', 'Happy Accidents', 'Liable to Floods' and 'Drinking with Hitler' all deal with war or conflict to some degree. What interests you about the ways in which Sheers presents war or conflict?

Taking it further ▶

Compare this version with the account of the same event in the poem in Sheers' *The Dust Diaries*, a non-fiction work in which he travels to Zimbabwe to write about his great-great-uncle, the missionary Arthur Cripps (Sheers, 2004, pp. 297–301).

The poem is more concerned with evoking feelings and emotions than telling a story

synaesthesia
a description in which one sensory impression is rendered in terms of another, as in 'a loud T-shirt' or 'a chilling voice'.

His final actions are theatrical: he 'leans in close' then makes an impressive exit by leaving quickly 'in a flourish of cards', which are presumably business cards and possibly an invitation for the Zambian woman to contact him.

The final stanza, however, presents Hunzvi as a distasteful character whose attentions were unwanted. As if tainted by his touch, the woman brushes the thigh where 'he laid his hand' and, with 'one slow blink of her blue-painted eyes', she seems to be 'washing him away'.

'Four Movements in the Scale of Two'

The poem presents four stages in a relationship. The first is a series of stylised images of a couple in bed in the morning; the second a series of delicate, near-abstract images of them touching; the third recounts a significant moment when something shocking was said by the woman; and in the final one, the moment of break-up is evoked by an extended image of a glass snapping under the water in a sink.

Commentary Stylistically, this is one of Sheers' most innovative poems. While many others narrate events clearly and evoke experiences tangibly, this one evokes moods and feelings in more abstract ways. Some aspects of the poem's use of enigmatic imagery might be compared with 'Night Windows' or 'Valentine', but it leaves more of its meaning for the reader to ponder. Indeed it might be argued that the poem is more concerned with evoking feelings and emotions than telling a story or conveying an idea. To some its enigmatic title might be reminiscent of modernist poetry. Like T. S. Eliot's *Four Quartets* (from which Sheers took the epigraph for *Skirrid Hill*), the title, 'Four Movements in the Scale of Two' is composed of musical terms: a symphony usually has four movements, or self-contained parts; a scale is a sequence of notes. While each 'movement' in Sheers' poem depicts an event in the same relationship, each one has a separate number and title as well as a different style. The first and the fourth are both in tercets and the middle two are in two-line stanzas.

'*I – Pages*' is a sequence of images that begins cinematically, we 'cut to … an overhead shot' of lovers 'Lying in bed, foetus curled'. The point of view is interesting in that the speaker is both an onlooker and a participant. Musical metaphors are occasioned by the image of the pair lying 'back to naked back': first they are 'opposing bass clefs', then 'elegant scars on the hips of a cello'. A sense of art and beauty continues as they metamorphose into the natural world as 'a butterfly's white wings'; after this, they grow more mysterious as they become 'the double heart of a secret fruit', then the unknown factor in a puzzle – the 'X in the equation' – before the movement ends on a self-referential note when they become the 'blank pages' of an open book. This seems a fitting image for a young relationship, and perhaps the series of inventive images that preceded it suggests that their life together promises many wonderful times ahead.

'*II – Still Life*' renders a moment of intimacy and does so primarily through 'a palette of touches'. This is an interesting and delicate use of **synaesthesia**, since Sheers uses one sense (sight) to convey another (touch). This continues as the language of art is used to tactile effect. For example, the woman's hair is 'shading' the man's shoulders with 'brushstrokes', and depth is added by the 'impression of [her] breasts'. Such details lead to a conclusion that uses 'touched' perhaps in two senses: of making physical contact and of provoking an emotional response, as the speaker deduces 'that bodies, like souls,/only exist when touched'.

Perhaps this moment, which takes place right at the middle of the poem, is the apex of the relationship, since the next, '*III – Eastern Promise*', offers an unexpected and dramatic climax. At first the title might suggest the allure of a woman from an exotic place – popular advertisements for Turkish Delight often featured a sultry woman in the desert and the tagline 'full of eastern promise' – but it turns out to have other connotations. The location of the east in this 'eastern promise' is much further away than we might have expected – not Turkey but Siberia, and perhaps the only promise is a broken one. Sheers builds tension in the movement's first two-line stanza – a complete sentence that presents the furtive image of the woman concealed beneath 'the dark tent of her down-falling hair' and the man's portentous request for her to speak. There is a greater distance between the speaker and the subject, which suits the coldness of this movement, as he recounts the experience as if it were happening to someone else. The remainder of it comprises three two-line stanzas that form a single sentence, in which thermal imagery and harsh-sounding consonants help to convey her chilling message that the relationship is over – a message that is not stated directly, but implied. The swirling sibilance of her 'summoning the Steppe and Siberian snow to their bed' underscores the sudden build-up of coldness, and contrasts starkly with the earlier artistic imagery of intimacy in movements I and II. Hard 'c' and 'k' sounds reinforce the impact of what is said, and the final image conveys an almost explosive sudden shift in temperature as the 'dropping' of the words is 'like the shock of new ice in old water'.

Just as a symphony's final movement often contains themes and motifs present earlier on, this poem's fourth movement, '*IV – Line-Break*', returns to the writing diction that was prominent in the first. But now there are no longer 'blank pages' suggesting youth and promise, but a line break, which suggests that the relationship has come to the point of completion. While it seems a momentous and disturbing end if we consider the shock of the previous movement and its chilling imagery, from the language of the final movement's second stanza it appears relatively trivial. The break-up is referred to as 'insignificant' and no more than 'a caesura' (a pause somewhere in the middle of a line of verse). Perhaps, while momentous when it happened, the break fades into insignificance through time, although that might only be possible when considering the experience in the cold light of logic and from the safe distance of hindsight. What stays with the reader are the arresting images of break-up and its effects, the final one of which depicts a musing moment of puzzlement at

TASK

Review the different types of poem that Sheers writes by thinking of different ways in which you might group them. You could draw up a list of the most enigmatic to the most straightforward, or the most narrative to the most purely emotional, or the most Welsh to the most international.

TASK

If you were asked to select one love poem from the collection as an appropriate introductory poem to Sheers' verse, which would you choose? Give reasons for your choice, making links to other poems in the collection.

Context

'Liable to Floods' was written for the Dolwyddelan Project in north Wales, in which all sorts of artists were 'taking the temperature of that area' (Sheers, 2006). Sheers wrote it when he heard of the American soldiers (often referred to as GIs), who were training for the D-day landings and ignored the local farmers who warned them that the area they were camping in was often affected by flash floods. Moel Siabod is the highest peak in the Moelwynion mountain range.

how it could have happened. The music of the lines helps to bring this free verse poem to an unsettling finale and, as the blood gathers slowly in the sink, so too do the effects of assonance, sibilance and rhyme as we consider the relationship that 'gave' like a snapped glass:

> that gives no sign it has done so
> until the slow smoke-signal of blood,
> uncurling from below.

There is a sense of the hidden nature of other people's feelings and the precarious nature of our relationships in this image. Like the glass, the language of love and relationships is largely beneath the surface. Like interpreting a smoke-signal, it can take patience and skill to read the signs. And, as the blood in the image implies, the consequences of breaking up, even if kept largely hidden, will be painful.

'Liable to Floods'

During the First World War, a Welsh farmer warns an American general that the area where he intends to set up a camp is liable to flood. The general carries on regardless. On the third night, heavy rainfall sweeps the camp away.

Commentary This poem tells a story of nature triumphing over technology. It seems to have the moral that you should never underestimate local knowledge or ignore the wisdom of those whose lives are spent working the land.

After the image-driven, modernist evocation of a relationship in 'Four Movements in the Scale of Two', this poem seems refreshingly straightforward: it progresses with an even pace in even quatrains that follow the rhythms of natural speech. It opens with dialogue and the farmer's warning that the area is 'liable to floods'. Like the father in 'Trees' who only says 'some time' when asked how long it will be before the trees are grown, the farmer says few words, but there is a sense of deep understanding lying beneath. Such understatement contrasts with the words of the general, who uses the American idiom 'We've got this one covered', which seems friendly, confident and possibly patronising. His words are accompanied by the cocky gesture of 'tipping back his cap with one finger' and the 'laying a fatherly hand on the farmer's shoulder'. The reader might suspect that this foreshadows trouble.

As the narrative progresses, the words 'On the third night' might strike readers as ominous, and the mood of the poem darkens as the style shifts from being straightforwardly narrative to being overtly figurative. The diction of war is used to evoke the effects of the weather: rain comes in a 'fusillade'; thunder is like 'artillery' and the river expands 'under cover of darkness'. The metaphorical language takes on a darker complexion as the river is 'bleeding through the camp' and floating cans and cups clink 'like ghosts in celebration'. Some might, however, read this simile as more comic than sinister and see the happy ghosts as the first sign of a joyful triumph of natural power over military arrogance.

Nature is personified as a woman in the eighth stanza, which forms a climax to the narrative. As with the earlier ghost image, there is a hint of humour as this woman performs diverse tasks from 'flushing out the latrines' to 'arming herself' with the soldiers' rifles. The final two stanzas offer a kind of coda to the action. Several of the soldiers have the same dawning consciousness that nature having taken over and 'swept away' the camp is somehow 'suitable'. As is typical with Sheers, poetic effects heighten his final thoughts; the repetition of 'this being' in the last two lines adds a rhetorical rhythm, and the use of a final couplet, rhyming 'without any say' with 'being swept away', ends the poem with a conclusive ring.

'History'

The speaker tells the reader not to go to a history book but a disused quarry to learn about north Wales. He instructs the reader to take a piece of slate, open it like a book and 'read' the real story of the place.

Commentary The poem is unusual in that it addresses the reader directly. History, the poem seems to argue, is not something that you read in a book, but something that you go out and experience. The narrative might be viewed as an act of primary historical research, in which the descriptive and sensuous language gives the impression of the reader/historian becoming immersed in the subject actively rather than reading about it passively.

Sheers' free verse is arranged into stanzas that are mostly quatrains, but these are interspersed with occasional two-line stanzas, which have the effect of encouraging the reader to focus on a detail, for example the song of the blackbird 'drilling its notes/into the hillside's soil'. A two-line stanza is used to render the moment of transformation when 'a blade of slate' becomes 'a book of slate'. This detail occurs at the climax of the narrative and it is from this book, not a history book, that one can read the 'story' that is 'written/throughout this valley'.

As in 'Liable to Floods', the poem closes with a resounding finish that uses both repetition and rhyme to heighten its impact. Parallelism and alliteration add a rhetorical ring — 'in every head, across every heart' — and by rhyming the last word, 'bone', with 'stone' from the second line of the penultimate stanza, Sheers adds a sonorous connection between the landscape and its people.

'Amazon'

The poem recounts four moments in the story of a woman who develops breast cancer, beginning with the discovery of the lump, then the diagnosis, then a family bonfire party that she attends shortly after her mastectomy, and finally an imagined trip to a swimming pool on nudist night.

TASK

Compare the ways in which Sheers presents nature in 'Liable to Floods' and 'Intermission'.

Context

Like the preceding one, this poem was written as part of the Dolwyddelan Project.

Taking it further ▶

'History' poem was published at the end of an article by Sheers in *Geography* entitled 'Poetry and place: some personal reflections' (Sheers, 2008). Use the link below to access the article. In what ways does it affect your response to Sheers' poems that deal with landscape? http://tinyurl.com/3lqq2rj

Context

Amazons were a legendary race of women, famed for their strength, height and athleticism, who, the ancient Greeks believed, lived at the edge of the known world. According to legend, it was normal for an Amazon woman to cut off her right breast so that she could hunt more proficiently with a bow.

Commentary The speaker does not claim full knowledge of his subject matter: he offers three possible ways for the woman to have discovered the cancerous growth. Perhaps, then, Sheers presents her as a composite figure rather than a specific person, which could be seen as a sensitive way for a male poet to tackle a subject that could be perceived as female.

The first section of this narrative poem ends ominously with a long line that describes the cancer, which is 'soft but hard as cartilage, and busy with its own beginning'. This sounds sinister, since the cancer is presented as a separate being, one that is active and has only just started to make its presence felt.

Sheers moves from tercets in the first section to two-line stanzas in the second. This slows down the narrative, making the reader pause and consider each moment. Rather than name the disease, Sheers has the woman ponder its sounds; she is surprised how language 'can carry so much chaos,/and how that word, with its hard C of cruelty' can seem so apt.

The reader is slowed by the alliteration and the stresses that fall on the hard 'c's as well as by the internal rhyme that links 'cruelty' and 'hard C'. The latter term may also, appropriately, remind readers of an informal (and euphemistic) way of referring to the disease – 'the big C'.

Context

Women have been inspired to fight against breast cancer by the stories surrounding the legends of the Amazons. For example, one support group has taken its name from them.

TASK

Consider the ways in which Sheers presents women in *Skirrid Hill*. Make notes on the different types of women and the different types of relationships with women that are depicted. Compare the different ways in which they are presented.

The next two-line stanza contrasts with the previous one, both in terms of its sounds and its shape on the page. After the long lines of the stanza that evoked the harshness and chaos of the disease, come these short lines: 'and soft c of uncertainty,/seems so fitted to the task'. The hardness of the previous consonant sounds has been replaced by soft sibilance, which might help to evoke the feelings of uncertainty that the diagnosis brings. The final part of this section deals with the paradox that while the woman's life has become so shatteringly different, the rest of the world remains 'startlingly the same'.

There is a temporal shift at the start of the next section. From details such as 'her first outing since' and the later mention of her entering the pool as an 'Amazon', we can deduce that the woman has undergone a mastectomy to remove the cancer. The occasion is Bonfire Night and the warmth and support of her family is evoked, particularly through the actions of her small son who presents her with a bottle of champagne. The sense of celebration and return to normal family life is offset by the knowledge of the seriousness of her disease, which may not have been eradicated completely. Sheers does this subtly with a tactile image as the feeling of the champagne cork, which is 'soft but hard, stubborn to the touch', merges into thoughts of the tumour.

Another time shift occurs in the final part of the poem. Its water imagery and sense of the female body are reminiscent of the first part and, as the woman reflects on her changed body, the perspective shifts to an imagined future in which she will visit the swimming pool on nudist night. This symbolises a complete return to confidence, and conveys a sense of empowerment that she will gain from showing her body without embarrassment. Such empowerment is emphasised by the final image which links to the poem's title, that of the one-breasted woman entering the water 'an Amazon'.

'Shadow Man'

The poem describes aspects of the work of the artist, Mac Adams. Assortments of typical still-life objects create, in shadow form, a dog, a bird or even a portrait of Karl Marx. The speaker reflects on a truth arising from the artist's working method: it is not the substance of things that count, but the effects that they have, 'the shadows they throw/against the lives of others'.

▲ *Portrait of Karl Marx* (1991) by Mac Adams

Commentary Composed of tercets of short lines, the poem's form suits its artistic subject matter and manages to evoke aspects of Adams' complex visual images using relatively simple words.

The first stanza announces the importance of light and shadow to the artist's work: his 'palette' does not contain colours, but different 'shades' of light. This subtle metaphor implies a magical quality to this man's creations, which is continued in the verb 'conjuring' positioned prominently at the beginning of the second stanza. This qualifies the nouns that are both the objects that help make his pictures, such as the 'bulb' and the 'fruit', and the shadow images that they help form, such as 'a bird's kinetic moment/in the second before flight' or 'Karl Marx's head'. These evocations of the images that Adams conjures make up three stanzas that are positioned prominently in the centre of the poem and are unified by being a single sentence.

The third and final part of the poem, which is also expressed in a single sentence, is what the speaker extrapolates from having considered the work of Adams. The sense of the magical continues, as the artist 'works with a darkness/behind his eyes' and seems blessed with an 'understanding' that is beyond that of other people, which the speaker expresses as it not being:

> matter that matters,
> or our thoughts and words,
> but the shadows they throw
>
> against the lives of others.

Despite such philosophical conclusions, some readers might liken his work and his insights to those of some of the characters in the first half of the collection that dealt with rural Wales. For example, there was also a numinous (spiritual or religious) quality to the work of the farrier and there was a paradoxically simple

Taking it further ▶

To view some of the shadow photographs of Mac Adams, visit his website http://macadamsstudio.com/#emptyspaces

You can view 'The Truce' by visiting:
http://en.museeniepce.com/index.php/exposition-en/exposition-passee/Mac-Adams

Scroll down to find 'The Truce'. The shadow sculpture of Karl Marx (which is evoked in the poem's fourth stanza) may be seen at www.uturn.org/Macadams/index.htm.

profundity in the words of the father who lost his son in 'The Hill Fort', who said that it wasn't 'the number of steps' that mattered but 'the depth of their impression'. Similarly, Adams' art does play with sculptures and shadows, but casts light in a more philosophical way. The conclusion of 'Shadow Man' seems to claim that our thoughts, words and actions are less important than the ways in which others perceive them, and this truth seems not just to apply to art, but to life.

Context

```
Mac Adams is a Welsh-born artist who lives and works in
New York. He is well known for his innovative sculptures
and photographs, in which objects cast unexpected shadows.
These shadows often form arresting images very unlike the
objects that produced them. For example, in 'The Truce'
(1999) straw, flowers, a vase and a jug produce shadow
images of two cats that have paused during a play fight.
```

'Under the Superstition Mountains'

The speaker and his companion, a photographer, rest in their car in Sun City West, where only the over-65s are allowed to own property. He describes the sights he sees: a man in a track-suit, walking with oxygen tanks in tow, a bird and, finally, his companion sleeping in the passenger seat beside him. He imagines a rattlesnake moving somewhere out of sight and shaking itself awake after hibernation.

Commentary This poem has a documentary feel, as the speaker seemingly responds to aspects of the environment around him. Tercets suit this style; they allow him to evoke a detail, or develop a thought concisely. The first image is of an iconic American car, a Mustang, which seems debased, since it is 'idle' and has only 'mock leather seats' and, like a horse whose working life is over, is 'out to grass'. Perhaps such details, like the epigraph, suggest the falseness that can lurk beneath the happy images of American life and foreshadow the poem's main concern, aspects of ageing.

The next detail, the speaker reading 'Lowell on marriage', suggests the ugliness that can lie behind the rosy façade of society's most fundamental institution, marriage. Lowell's 'To speak of the woe that is in marriage' is a sonnet, written in the persona of a wife who complains of her drunken, argumentative and prostitute-using husband.

The details that follow seem less sinister, if a little strange. The speaker tells the reader that the town in which he sits parked is 'where only the old are allowed to live' and, in the fourth stanza, he describes 'a man in a track-suit' who 'takes his oxygen tanks for a walk'. In the passenger seat, the photographer becomes another image of old age, as he is 'sedated by the heat' and sleeps with 'his finger on the trigger/of the shutter, as if he'd died/and finally shot the perfect still'.

Context

The epigraph is from the song 'Susan's House' by the American rock group Eels. It is ironic, since the white picket fence might be said to be an iconic image of wholesome, suburban America, yet the song goes on to evoke images of insanity, arson, death by shooting, drug pushing and teenage pregnancy. Perhaps by choosing such an epigraph, Sheers is preparing readers for the strangeness of the America that he describes in the poem.

Taking it further ▶

Use a search engine to find a recording or a video of the song by Eels, quoted in the epigraph, or try www.youtube.com/watch?v=ovEPEzcAlW0.

Perhaps the next stage after having built a community solely for the old is hinted at in the poem's final image, since it is one of rejuvenation, even rebirth. Recapturing youth is not yet a part of this world – it takes place 'somewhere off camera' – and this is not presented as an intelligent approach to growing old. The rattlesnake awakes after hibernation and 'shakes itself alive, without knowing why'.

We might compare the bizarre images of growing old in this poem with the healthy acceptance of ageing in the collection's poems that are set in Wales, for example in the father's attitude in 'Trees' or the dignified deaths in 'On Going' and 'The Wake'.

'Service'

The speaker invites the reader to imagine the activities inside a prestigious restaurant, from the earliest arrivals of produce to clearing-up time after the final sitting.

Commentary Using free verse and irregular stanzas, 'Service' follows the rhythms of the day at a restaurant. It has the feeling of an unscripted radio commentary or documentary in which the presenter responds honestly and directly to the events going on around him. Like a performance poem, it uses the rhythms of speech and techniques such as listing and repetition to sweep the reader along by the energy of what is being described.

Context

Sheers wrote this poem and 'Hedge School' as a commission for National Poetry Day 2004 while he was poet-in-residence at the Fat Duck, Bray. The theme that year was food. It is perhaps one of his most accessible poems, and, given its loose form, its pace and immediacy, it is hardly surprising that at readings it is often greeted by spontaneous applause.

Context

Sheers wrote 'Under the Superstition Mountains' while in America with the photographer David Hearn, who was working on a project on ageing. This took them to Sun City West, which is underneath the Superstition Mountains in Arizona. You have to be at least 65 years old to buy property there. As Sheers sat looking up at the mountain range the experience got him thinking 'about different forms of ageing' (Sheers, 2006).

While the poem has a linear structure, there is also a cyclical effect as the sommelier who tastes wine at the beginning of the day returns to this work in the last stanza, suggesting that while a meal at the restaurant might be a theatrical event for the diners, for those who work there each day it follows a familiar cycle. The split between diners and workers might also be present in the title: service can be the shout of a chef for the waiters to collect food, or a kind of ceremony (which a meal at a very fine restaurant often is), but it can also refer to the work done by waiters or even the state of being employed as a servant.

▲ Heston Blumenthal, chef-proprietor of The Fat Duck. Sheers was his poet-in-residence in 2004

The poem begins with a four-line prose-like prologue, which instructs the reader or listener to 'imagine a theatre'; it then goes on to supply the visual and aural images of 'a lone Hoover' that 'hums' picking up 'what's left of last night'. This opening serves to whet the reader's appetite for what is to follow, and, after details of deliveries, a sense of occasion is conveyed by the description of the tables and their tablecloths which are compared to 'girls at a prom dress fitting'. After describing this part of the 'set', Sheers turns to one of the actors, the sommelier. In the sixth stanza the extended metaphor of the theatre is discarded in favour of likening the kitchen to a submarine, which is perfect for conveying the bustle of activity in a confined space involving skilled people who must work as part of a hierarchical team.

Much of the joy of this poem is in the evocation of the food. As when describing other kinds of art or artful pursuits – such as the work of Mac Adams or the farrier, or even the use of make-up in 'Show' – Sheers presents the work in the kitchen as a type of magic: onion puree is mixed in a 'witch's cauldron' and salted pork is 'hung in the water bath/like a regular Houdini'. The descriptions of food preparation also demonstrate the precision and skill of the cooks. Sheers describes intricate operations, such as opening a sea bass 'with one score of the knife', which then has 'its bones unstitched with a pliers'; he goes on to use metaphor to convey colour and temperature and appeal to the reader's sense of taste as the boned sea bass becomes a 'pink blank page/waiting for nothing/but heat and the tongue'.

This metaphor is typical of Sheers' use of diction and imagery drawn from the world of writing. For example, he also uses a simile of salmon being 'piled

Sheers presents the work in the kitchen as a type of magic

TASK

Compare the ways in which food is presented in 'Service' and 'Oysters' by Heaney.

high like the deckle-edged leaves/of a medieval manuscript'. This conveys the preciousness of the salmon, the skill of those who prepared them and their shape (since they lie, on top of each other, like the pages of an old book – deckle edges are the ragged fringes on handmade paper). As the food is ready to leave the kitchen, the chef is presented as 'an author, copy-editing the text'. Copy-editing is the final editing stage before publication and does not usually involve altering the text substantially; it is more concerned with checking for aspects such as clarity and consistency. Accordingly, Sheers' metaphor elevates cooking to the level of art and implies that there are rigorous processes in a good kitchen, where the chef is the 'author' of the food, giving each plate his approval before it is released into the dining room.

The artistry of the kitchen contrasts with the ease of the dining room. The first diner is referred to metonymically as 'a suit' and the 'globe of his stomach' over which he unfurls a napkin is also compared to 'a sail tacking tight above his belt,/already on the last notch'. Perhaps this depiction represents the restaurant's typical customer as being faceless, greedy and rich. Indeed some readers might argue that, beneath the dazzling display of fine food and culinary skill, there is an implied criticism of the ways in which so many are engaged in 'service' to meet the needs of so few. Such a view might be substantiated by the efforts of the 'solitary Scottish diver' in the North Sea whose labours help to bring the finest oysters to the tables of the rich, or in Sheers' depiction of the restaurant's sommelier. The sommelier, who is responsible for wine, might be thought to have a desirable job: he would have a detailed knowledge of wine, much of which would have come from having tasted many fine wines himself. Yet Sheers presents this most exquisite of jobs as a tough, working-class pursuit. He 'spits/a boxer's mouthful of red': the sommelier spitting wine is like a boxer spitting blood. The poem returns to the sommelier in its final stanza, perhaps adding to the feeling that working life at the restaurant is cyclical, or – as might be suggested by the cleaning activities that envelop the events of the poem – even routine. The sommelier is characterised as performing working-class actions, first as a darts player, holding his 'arrow' by the stem, then as a gardener 'scenting his rose'.

'The Fishmonger'

The speaker describes a fishmonger, detailing his actions in taking a carp from a bucket, his toughness and his skill with a knife. Cold-hearted, he could cut up a man with the same skill if he had to fight.

Commentary An adaptation of a work by the Hungarian poet, István László, 'The Fishmonger' takes the subject of the original but alters some aspects of the subject matter and imagery and changes the form. The Hungarian poem is a single 22-line stanza in free verse; Sheers also uses free verse, but renders the experience in seven tercets that slow the action and give images greater prominence.

Taking it further ▷

Why not find out more about the restaurant and the chef who helped to inspire the poem? Go to www.thefatduck.co.uk.

CRITICAL VIEW

'In poems such as "Hedge School", "Service" and "The Fishmonger", Sheers is, above all, interested in exploring the sensual and indulgent aspects of eating.' How far do you agree with this statement?

Context

'The Fishmonger' was commissioned as part of the British Council's 'Converging Lines' project to coincide with Hungary joining the EU in 2004.

TASK

Compare 'The Fishmonger' to Antony Dunn's translation of the poem, 'Fishmonger'. You can find this poem and more information about István László at **http://tinyurl. com/3bkdrqo.**

zeugma a figure of speech in which one verb governs two nouns or phrases, conveying two distinct actions.

The opening line suggests that the subject may not be a particular person but a type. That the era is 'the age of the fishmonger not the fisherman' might lead some to wonder why this ostensibly low-status job has been elevated to the defining role of the era. We might wonder if the poem is a comment on developing capitalism, where the producer is no longer the controlling force, but only the seller. The seller depicted in Sheers' poem is cold-hearted and dangerous. Indeed the whole poem shadows the figure of the fishmonger with a sinister murkiness, suggesting his brutal and deadly fighting prowess. The final line of the first stanza shows him looking at his customers, but sizing them up and 'measuring their movements' as though readying himself for combat. The fish he lifts effortlessly from a bucket is a carp – usually a dangerous fighting fish – and the oxymoronic 'cruel kindness' suggests that he kills it with speed.

The subject of the fourth stanza is ambiguous: we have just been thinking of carp, but now it seems that the 'flesh' being cut is human. This thought develops in the fifth stanza as we learn how the fishmonger understands how to 'pare his speech as he might men'. The use of **zeugma** is sinister: it suggests that he can cut open a man as easily as he can choose to speak concisely. The final images are ones of violence and heartlessness: like a lightning-struck tree 'there is no healing bark' about his heart. Sheers connects this tree image with a fish image, providing a cyclical effect in the final two lines as the tree trunk's gasps for growth are likened in a dramatic image to 'a fish/struggling for its last breath as if biting the air for water'.

'Stitch in Time'

An Indian tailor leaves his young wife to travel in search of work. When he makes a suit for a chief in Fiji he is given an acre of land, which is exactly on the antemeridian, the line of longitude exactly 180 degrees both east and west of the prime meridian.

Ten years later, he returns for his wife and she sees the businesses that he founded, all of which bear the name 'Meridian'. When the family go to London the first place he visits is Greenwich.

Commentary The title is appropriate for a poem about a tailor, since it comes from the proverb 'a stitch in time saves nine'. This originally advised mending a small hole in a garment quickly, rather than leaving it until later, when the hole would have become bigger and would need nine extra stitches. The proverb, therefore, has come to mean that effort spent resolving a problem saves time in the long run. Perhaps in this context it refers to the tailor's time spent in Fiji making his fortune, which was preferable to spending many more years labouring in poverty in India.

'Stitch in Time' is a narrative poem that begins towards the end of its story. The opening – 'And so he left his wife' – sounds as though the reader is beginning to hear the story after a large part of it has already been told. Sheers uses tailoring diction throughout, and the metaphor of the 'chalk mark' is used to suggest the invisible line of longitude on which the tailor's land is situated. (Chalk lines, which can be removed easily, are often made on garments to guide processes such as stitching and cutting.)

In keeping with the poem's sense of balance – the 180-degree meridian is a half-way point on the earth – Sheers uses couplets, albeit loose ones, whose rhymes (or half-rhymes) do not intrude on the poem's narrative flow. A particularly strong rhyme marks the end of the poem's first part, at the end of the eighth stanza, when the tailor receives the piece of land that is to determine the rest of his life. This stanza is also rhythmically very regular, and it closes this part of the story with an appropriate resonance. There is wry humour about its location. Since it lies on the International Date Line (the 180-degrees meridian), it marks where 'today is ending' and 'tomorrow starts'. The rhymes grow stronger after the tailor gains both the land and a guiding principle in his life.

The language of tailoring and the influence of the meridian are both resurgent at the poem's close. As an old man in London 'his joints were as stiff as his oldest scissors'; even looking at the sky 'where the swallows darted' recalls his trade, since a 'dart' can be a type of stitching that forms a tuck in a garment. Again, the final thought of the poem characterises the Greenwich Meridian as not only 'the source, the still point after the strife' but also 'the first stitch in the pattern to which he'd cut his life'.

'L.A. Evening'

The speaker describes a woman at the end of a day looking at some photographs from her life as an actor, before she tends to her dog and cats and prepares for bed.

Commentary The poem is a vignette in which the speaker narrates a third person account of some moments of an actress shortly before bedtime. The time of day – evening – seems to be symbolic, as the woman seems to have reached old age. The subject appears to be Jean Simmons (1929–2010), the British actress who starred alongside actors such as Marlon Brando in *Guys and Dolls* and Laurence Olivier in *Hamlet*. The third person perspective and the lack of overt emotion in the poem lend it a detached mood. Readers might see Simmons as a lonely, even reclusive figure. She seems isolated from the Los Angeles in which she lives. All the activity appears to be taking place outside her house: the 'sirens', the 'rollerbladers' and even the sunset. There is a lack of movement inside and, even when she sits to a 'screening', the pictures that she sees are not moving, but old 'photographs'. Perhaps there is the sense that these photographs of her former life are, paradoxically, more real than the actual life that she lives at present. This is also suggested by Sheers' use of form, since the two central stanzas that evoke the past are both sestets and a line longer than the five-line stanzas that frame this experience of viewing the photos.

The epigraph adds a further note of melancholy, since it quotes the acclaimed classical actor and theatre manager, E. Booth (perhaps actually Edwin rather

Taking it further

You can begin research on the 180th meridian and the International Date Line by visiting http://tinyurl.com/3nhgcxl.

Taking it further

You can discover more about Jean Simmons by visiting http://tinyurl.com/ykefxzq.

Jean Simmons in
Laurence Olivier's film
version of *Hamlet* (1948) ▶

than 'Edward'), who was said to have heard from 'the god of all arts' that he would bring elation and despair, but perhaps, most cruelly, the recipient of fame would never know when it would be granted or taken away. The loss of fame is not depicted as a dramatic reversal of fortunes, however. Rather there seems to be a mood of nostalgia, loneliness or even ennui. Looking at the photographs is presented as a habitual action – 'as always she leaves/before the roll call of the credits' – just like checking her animals. The rhyme at the end of the poem, in lines three and five of the final stanza, seems to emphasise the mundaneness of her current life: turning the 'dimmer switch into the night' then checking the 'sensitivity of the intruder light'. The 'light' takes us back to 'night', closing the poem on a muted if not gloomy note, and contrasting with the happiness of the other full rhyme in the poem which linked two moments of extreme success: meeting with the queen 'mother and daughter' and being swung by Brando in *Guys and Dolls* 'as if he'd just caught her'.

'The Singing Men'

Buskers are the subject of this poem. The speaker reflects on the lives they once had, then lists some of the places in which they may be found, before focusing on a single opera singer who performs to commuters in Balham tube station.

Commentary The fleeting, insubstantial sense evoked by the unrhymed two-line stanzas is apt for the subject of the ubiquitous busker. The poem might be seen as divided into two halves: the first half (which comprises five stanzas and four sentences) considers buskers in general and the shared aspects of the busking lifestyle; the second half deals with some of the particular types of busker. This second part is written in a single meandering sentence, which might be seen as appropriate for describing those whose lives are unstructured and loose. The songs they sing in different places seem to represent some of life's most powerful emotions: love, as heard in the 'ballads on the Staten Island ferry' (although the use of the verb 'toting' might also make some think of violence since 'gun' usually collocates with 'toting'); lamentation, as heard in the 'slave songs in New Jersey'; togetherness, as heard in the folk songs in Moscow; and sadness, as heard singing the 'blues in Leeds'.

Sheers avoids sentimentalising the singers; he simply describes. Perhaps there is something admirable in the way in which they can sing despite their worries, and Sheers seems to suggest that there is something universal – and male – about the busking experience: men do it everywhere from New Jersey to Moscow. Perhaps their omnipresence and the kind of (mostly sad) songs they sing suggest that there is something necessary, even cathartic, about hearing them.

The final image in the poem's meandering last sentence is of a single busker in Balham. He encapsulates some of the complexities and contradictions of his art. His busking spot is **liminal** – 'on the edge of the underground' – and perhaps suggests the subterranean or surreptitious nature of his existence. In this very ordinary setting he practises one of the most elitist arts, opera. Despite his costume being 'perfect', he looks uncared for, with his 'beard scribbled over his chin' and his ironically named 'gold can of Extra', which carries associations of alcoholism. While there is something comforting about his arias welcoming the commuters, there is also something poignant for this **deracinated** singer in the poem's final word: 'home'.

Sheers characterises the buskers as liminal figures, who hover on the margins of society, in 'corners and doorways' or 'on the edges of things'. In the centre of the poem comes the suggestion of what they might have been previously: people who lived normal lives with normal social connections – people who had wives, children and possibly lovers. Yet what was once peripheral to them – 'a little music' – has become central.

TASK
Consider the ways in which Sheers uses photographs, or images from photography or cinematography, in his poems. Some of the poems that you might choose to explore include 'L.A. Evening', 'Under the Superstition Mountains', 'Four Movements in the Scale of Two' and 'Happy Accidents'.

liminal marginal; in a state of transition; occupying a position on, or near, a boundary.

deracinate to uproot a person from their native environment or culture.

'The Wake'

The speaker's dying grandfather tells him that he does not want his life to be prolonged. When he has shown the speaker to the door, the speaker feels a sense of his passing; it is as if a ship has gone by and the water has been disturbed at the sides but has settled at the rear.

Commentary After four poems set in far-flung places, Sheers returns to the homely and familial in this penultimate poem of the collection. It is written from a more intimate and involved perspective than most in the last half of the collection, in which the speaker is typically an observer. The poem is an elegy for the poet's grandfather, who was a chest consultant and served in the Royal Navy during the Second World War. These two elements unite to provide the imagery at the start of the poem that depicts his illness and his response to it; he does not want the doctor to 'plumb … the depths of his scarred lungs'. This reminds the speaker of his grandfather's work treating the chest problems of others: lungs are presented as 'pale oceans,/rising and falling in the rib cage's hull'.

The poem conveys the difficulty of communication through a nautical metaphor: the speaker says what he 'can', but his 'words are spoken/into a coastal wind long after the ship has sailed'. The sense is that the words are not completely what he wanted to say, just what he could; the idea of their inadequacy is continued by their being spoken into not just a wind, but a 'coastal wind', which is stronger, and after the listener has stopped paying attention.

The conceit of the grandfather as a ship continues in the next stanzas, but, by contrast, emphasising not the difficulties of dying, but the majesty of the man and the magnitude of his passing. It is 'later', and the perspective shifts subtly from the 'I' and 'he' of the earlier stanza, when verbal communication failed, to 'we', when both people understand the significance of what is happening without using words. The 'frame' of the doorway in which the grandfather stands is symbolic of the threshold between life and death. The speaker understands the impact that his grandfather's death will have on the family: his passing will leave a 'wake as that of a great ship/that disturbs the sea for miles'. The importance of this thought, which occurs at the climax of the poem's narrative, is underlined by its use of the poem's title, which readers will understand as meaning not only a 'wake', as in a ritual or party held directly after someone has died, but also the trail of water left after the passage of a ship.

The final three stanzas explore the consequences of the grandfather's passing, but suggest hope as much as sorrow. The disturbed sea 'for miles either side' might suggest the impact of the grandfather's life and the mark he has made on the community at large, while the fact that the passing leaves 'the water directly at its stern/strangely settled, turned, fresh/and somehow new' might suggest that those closest to him are thankful that the pain of dying is over and are coming to accept their new lives without their loved

CRITICAL VIEW

'In *Skirrid Hill* the most powerful representations of masculinity are brutal and unappealing.' Examine this view of the collection.

TASK

Compare the ways in which Heaney in *Field Work* and Sheers in *Skirrid Hill* present masculinity.

one. Sheers moves fluidly from the metaphor of the water to develop a simile using the sea, which encompasses both past and future. The movement caused by the wake is like:

> the first sea there ever was
>
> or that ever will be.

As in earlier familial poems, such as 'Trees' and 'On Going', 'The Wake' shows the individual's life as being connected to the community or to life in general; life is characterised as a process that does not end with a single person's death. The poem ends on a note of hope that is reinforced by the resounding internal rhyme, which unites past and future by its emphasis on 'the first sea' and 'ever will be'.

'Skirrid Fawr'

The speaker reflects on being drawn back to the Skirrid. He considers the view and the physical aspects of the hill, which resemble the features of a person or a horse.

Commentary Written in free verse and comprising eight unrhymed two-line stanzas, the poem describes the Skirrid and suggests aspects of its significance. It is sometimes known as 'Holy Mountain' or 'Sacred Hill' and this aspect of the place is seen in the first two stanzas as the speaker is drawn back to this place for answers 'just like the farmers' who scooped soil from 'her holy scar'. Hills are often seen as holy places or places of enlightenment. For example, Mohammed went into a cave on Mount Hira in which he received revelations that would become the Qur'an and Moses went to Mount Sinai where he received the Ten Commandments. The Skirrid is personified as a woman, and its ridge is referred to as 'her broken spine'. It is here to which the speaker goes in search of 'the answers/to every question' he has 'never known'. This is reminiscent of the power of the landscape in 'Y Gaer (*The Hill Fort*)', where the land seen from on top of the hill was 'three-sixty' and offered 'an answer to any question'. Although 'the blunt wind glancing from her withers' in 'Skirrid Fawr' is less extreme than the punishing weather in the earlier poem, it is perhaps this proximity to the elements that helps provide 'the answers'.

Taking it further ▷

To find out more about the Skirrid and some of the legends associated with it, go to

- www.nationaltrust.org.uk/sugarloaf-and-usk-valley/features/skirrid-myths-and-legends
- https://en.wikipedia.org/wiki/Ysgyryd_Fawr
- www.llanddewiskirrid.co.uk/skirrid/skirrid.htm

The hill is, however, not presented as being idyllic. Although Sheers provides his readers with a picture-postcard image of 'part hill, part field,/rising from a low mist', the edge that is emerging from this has a 'cleft palate'. There is a sense too that, perhaps like the prophesies of the Delphic oracle, the answers given from this high place might be ambiguous or contradictory: this beautiful hill seems, on first reading, to be quintessentially Welsh, yet it is described as being 'a lonely hulk,/adrift through Wales'. And if the poem seems to begin with a question, it appears to end not with an answer, but with a further question. 'Her weight' might appear to be her gravitas – her heavy and imposing qualities – but this could be interpreted to convey the weight of expectation that the place confers upon the speaker. Going to this numinous and impressive place makes him feel both a part of Wales and apart from Wales since he lacks fluency in Welsh, his 'unlearned tongue'.

This final image might also remind us of the very first poem – the broken landscape of 'Mametz Wood' and the 'absent tongues' of the dead soldiers. 'Skirrid Fawr' also, of course, evokes the collection's title, and reprises other elements from earlier poems. For example, the hill is the one that was climbed early in the collection in 'Farther', and the power of the landscape that it suggests is also evoked in many poems from 'Liable to Floods' to 'Trees'. Elements of language, such as the diction of writing, which we see in 'Skirrid Fawr' in phrases like 'the sentence of her slopes' and 'her vernacular of borders' have been used in a variety of other poems such as 'Border Country', 'Marking Time' and 'Amazon'. And the sense of splitting, or separation (suggested by aspects such as 'her broken spine', 'her east-west flanks' and the poem's paradoxical close) is evoked in many of the other poems that are concerned with personal separations or transitional states, such as the passage from adolescence to adulthood, or from life to death.

TASK

Read the interview with Owen Sheers at **www.poetryarchive. org**. Search on 'Poets', then 'Sheers', and from his page follow the link to the interview.

Note what he says about Welsh identity. To what extent do you feel that this is a major concern in the collection?

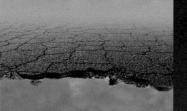

Themes

Target your thinking

- What subjects or issues do the poems address; what ideas do they raise or explore? (**AO1**)
- How might your appreciation of the poems' themes and concerns be shaped by your understanding of contexts? (**AO3**)
- If relevant to your exam board, which themes do the Sheers poems and your comparative text share? In what ways might you make thematic connections? (**AO4**)
- In what ways might understanding more about themes open up alternative interpretations of the poems? (**AO5**)

Themes may be thought of as the major concerns that the author addresses in the text: the topics or issues that the writer wants to explore. Thinking in terms of themes is a useful way to group your thoughts, and you may wish to subdivide a large theme into smaller sub-groups. A literary text, however, is not a simple, unilateral form of communication that seeks to transmit a straightforward message; readers, reviewers and critics often disagree on exactly what constitute a text's main concerns. Even the author's views on this may not be fixed. Accordingly, you will notice that themes are not discrete aspects, but are often connected; and part of the poet's skill is that he can often explore several interlinked themes simultaneously.

More specifically, Sheers' major themes might be seen in his choice of title and epigraph. 'Skirrid', as is noted at the beginning of the book, is 'from the Welsh *Ysgyrid*' and means 'divorce or separation'. We might, therefore, consider **moments of separation** – not only in the context of **relationships**, but also through **adolescence** and **death** – as themes. The choice of a Welsh place-name (even if it has been anglicised) might suggest that aspects of Wales, perhaps the Welsh **landscape** or Welsh **identity**, will also be thematic concerns. The epigraph – 'As we grow older/The world becomes stranger, the pattern more complicated/Of dead and living' – also suggests Sheers' themes: most obviously, adolescence and dying; but perhaps the strangeness and complexity mentioned in the epigraph also suggest Sheers' thematic interests in **war** and the **strangeness of the wider world**. The words in the Eliot poem that precede the part that Sheers quotes – 'Home is where one starts from' – might suggest another theme that is especially prominent in the first half of *Skirrid Hill*, the **family**.

Note that the suggested themes that follow are intended to provide you with some models for grouping the poems thematically. They are not intended as an all-encompassing checklist. All of the emboldened words above could also be used as thematic headings and there are many other suggestions for linking the poems throughout the commentaries part of this guide. Be flexible in your thinking and be prepared to suggest themes and groupings of your own.

Family

Family relationships are a source of strength in Sheers' poetry, from 'Inheritance', which acknowledges the debts he owes to his parents (and perhaps to the Welsh poets who have gone before him), to 'On Going', 'The Wake' and 'Amazon', which evoke feelings of love and show the bravery of loved ones who are suffering. These tender poems do not just celebrate individuals but also suggest their connectedness to their family or their wider community. In contrast to poems like 'The Singing Men' and 'L.A. Evening', there is something wholesome and grounded about these depictions of family life. Many of the poems in the early part of the collection present familial relationships in the context of nature. For example, the closeness of father and son is enhanced by a walk up the Skirrid in 'Farther' and the planting in 'Trees' is used to evoke a sense of one generation moving on while another grows to take its place.

Yet some troubling lessons are also learned in the context of family relationships. The cruelty that seems to be part of masculinity – as witnessed in poems such as 'Hedge School' – is also seen in 'Late Spring' when the speaker feels 'like a man' by helping his grandfather castrate lambs. Perhaps the most troubling poem amongst those set in the homely environment of rural Wales is 'Border Country', and here the source of the trouble lies not outside, but within, the family. Death comes not through age or illness, but suicide, and while its underlying causes are not specified, the effects of the farmer's violent death are seen at the end of the poem, through his son, who, both literally and metaphorically, has lost his way.

Adolescence

The separation between childhood and adulthood is one of the prominent types of rupture presented in *Skirrid Hill*. 'Hedge School' narrates a rural tale of burgeoning manhood and its concomitant desires for excess and violence. Masculinity is also explored, in a slightly more urban setting, by the poem on the opposite page, 'Joseph Jones', where the form of maleness on display is no more attractive. Jones pumps his body with press-ups, preens his hair with gel and scents his face with aftershave in order to be attractive on nights out. He is vain, boastful and his main accomplishments appear to be womanising, drinking and fighting. Although there is also pathos in Sheers' presentation: he once had a trial for Cardiff Youth, and, after the shared jokes about him, the recollections of the man in the bar who narrates the poem fade into fragments. Perhaps we might pity Jones – who might stand for many young Welsh men – or bemoan a culture that offers few ways for a young man to assert his masculinity.

The poem that follows 'Joseph Jones', 'Late Spring', provides a contrasting version of growing up, once more in a rural context. Specific details of the processes of castrating lambs and tail docking, it seems, show a kind of brutality that is a necessary part of being a farmer and being a man. There is a disturbing sense of becoming a man in this poem, not just in the surreal imagery at the end, but also in the way that manly work seems to involve an inversion of natural, nurturing processes. The 'harvest' that is the fruit of the male labour is nothing that will nourish, only the evidence of what it has destroyed.

While most of the poems of growing up depict normal rites of passage, others suggest adolescence cut short. For example, a sense of an accelerated adolescence is seen in 'Mametz Wood', in which Sheers depicts the 'wasted young'; and 'Border Country' tells the story of a boy who was pitched 'without notice,/through the windscreen' of his 'youth'. Unlike the descriptions of castration, or the gory details of Jones' sexual exploits, the boy's actions in the transitional state of adolescence are suggested rather than stated. The violent event alluded to in the car crash metaphor is the suicide of his father, which casts a pall over the whole poem, both before and after the event is narrated. For example, when he plays in the abandoned car as a boy he is 'going nowhere'; this evokes the purposelessness of his life after his father's death. Also, the names of the cars are described as 'the names of the dead'. Images of nothingness, decay and shrinkage lend an elegiac mood: the cars' speedos are 'settled at zero', their colours are 'rusting to red', the cars are 'smaller' and the whole place is 'diminished'. The boy's horizons have been narrowed; and while his adolescence has been forcedly accelerated, it seems his adult drive and sense of direction have been lost.

Wales and Welsh identity

Much of the collection is set in Wales. Poems of the Welsh landscape are positioned prominently. For example, the companion poems 'Y Gaer (*The Hill Fort*)' and 'The Hill Fort (*Y Gaer*)' are at the collection's mid-point and 'Skirrid Fawr' at the conclusion. All of these poems suggest that there is something restorative in the Welsh landscape. The Skirrid offers the 'answers/to every question' in 'Skirrid Fawr'; it provides the backdrop for a picture of two generations and their growing closeness in 'Farther'; and, when times are hard, the Iron Age hill fort in 'Y Gaer' supplies 'something huge enough to blame'. The landscape is also a symbol for life continuing and for family and community being bigger than individuals. This is made explicit in 'Trees', where there is a sense of the father accepting his decline and looking forward to his son's rise. The broader vantage point attained by a hilltop perspective is also seen in 'The Hill Fort (*Y Gaer*)', where the man who lost his son looks out over places such as 'Tretower, Raglan' and 'Bredwardine' and recognises comfortingly that 'in these generations/we're no more than scattered grains'.

It would be difficult, though, to argue that Sheers' poems define a typical Welsh identity – rather, his poems present several varieties of Welshness. The

Context

Sheers acknowledges that when re-reading his finished work 'it is almost impossible not to travel back through your own work detecting the shared territories, themes and preoccupations that may exist even if you didn't place them there when writing the individual poems' (Sheers, 2008, p.31).

In Sheers' article on the collection, he comments that 'although none of the poems in the book are in the Welsh language I feel that all my poetry, as I am in a way, is "derived from the Welsh"' (Sheers, 2008, p. 31). Can you explain what you think he means, giving examples from the poems?

autobiographical poems that explore family life in a Welsh context tend to be the warmest and those with the most secure sense of identity. For example, 'Inheritance' evokes Sheers' Welsh background, through details such as the 'hill's bare bones', the 'chaos of bad weather' and 'moments beside a wet horse'; such elements contribute to the poet's stable sense of his identity and heritage – which includes his Welsh literary heritage, given that the poem is '*After R. S. Thomas*'. Other poems, such as 'On Going', communicate a stable identity in the sense of being part of an ongoing family and, in the cases of 'Trees', 'The Equation' and 'Farther', a sense that being at one with the Welsh landscape is part of this sense of belonging.

As we move outwards from the stable family unit and the secure sense of identity that it brings, Sheers depicts aspects of Welsh experience that are much less cosy. For example, the poems of growing up present a potential for violence accompanying nascent manhood. Thus, in 'Hedge School' we have the desire for blackberries being portrayed as bloodlust, and the lesson that the countryside teaches the boy is 'just how dark he runs inside'. Perhaps the small rural communities can be oppressive as well as liberating. The eponymous Joseph Jones might have once been notorious in his Welsh community, but, by the end of the poem, his identity seems to have faded into a few memories of some of the things that once defined him:

> XR2,
>> late night fights,
>>> a trial once with Cardiff Youth.

Perhaps after the failure of his sporting career, life in 'a small town' with limited opportunities left him with only destructive outlets for his male identity.

The darker side of the life of Welsh rural communities is seen in 'Border Country', 'Y Gaer' and 'The Hill Fort'. All three deal with the effects of death. While the causes of the suicide in the 'Border Country' are unspecified, the poem might make readers think of some of the difficulties of living in rural farming communities, where, for example, the impact of diseases such as foot-and-mouth, of changes in farming subsidies or disputes over legacies after the landowner has died might have deleterious effects on mental health. Whatever the causes of the suicide, the poem shows the effects not just on the immediate victim, but also on the son who must make sense of his father's violent death. Similarly, 'Y Gaer' and 'The Hill Fort' do not specify the cause of the boy's death at the age of 19, but might make us think of issues such as death through traffic accidents, perhaps caused by young drivers in fast cars, like Joseph Jones in his XR2.

In the latter half of the collection two poems deal with Welsh identity at a broader, and more depressing, level. In 'Flag' we see images of flagging Welsh pride and 'The Steelworks' offers a bleak picture of the town that once produced the most steel in Europe, but which now only produces men who pump iron.

Taking it further ▷

You can find out more about the impact of the foot-and-mouth outbreak in Wales by visiting bbc.co.uk at http://tinyurl.com/3uzntwl.

The wider world

It would be a mistake to see Sheers solely as a Welsh poet. The war poems show him engaging with the wider world, but there are others that deal with the strangeness of life in far-off places. For example, the unusual payment of land on the International Date Line is the catalytic event in the story of the Meridian businesses in 'Stitch in Time' and the unusual requirements for property ownership in Sun City West provoke the interest of the speaker and his photographer friend in 'Under the Superstition Mountains'. An original Hungarian poem provides the source for a sinister portrait of a man of violence in Sheers' adaptation, 'The Fishmonger', while other poems from outside his Welsh homeland provide platforms for him to explore aspects of contemporary life. For example, 'L.A. Evening' engages with the early-twenty-first century obsession with fame by presenting an elegiac portrait of an actress who lives alone and seems to lead a lonely existence now that her co-stars are dead and the most alive things she has left are her memories. While set closer to home, 'Service' also engages with a contemporary preoccupation, cookery, and captures the brilliance and perfectionism of the three-star chef, while suggesting subtly the divisions between those who eat and those who work in the restaurant.

War and conflict

Sheers' poems that deal with conflict are concerned with its lasting effects and the ways in which we remember the past. Even a poem that is in many ways humorous, 'Liable to Floods', is an act of remembrance since it records an item of oral history. The climax of its story, when the floods sweep away the American camp, seems to suggest that nature is opposed to warfare – something that might also be taken from 'Mametz Wood', in which the earth containing the bodies of the soldiers allows them to rise, like a wound working foreign bodies 'to the surface of the skin'. There is a gruesome sense of war and its unnaturalness in this poem too – most memorably at its macabre climax when we picture the skeletons of the soldiers, which appear to be singing and are linked as if participating in a dance of death.

There is little overt sense of causes or politics in Sheers' war poems; typically the reader is invited not to apportion blame for violence, but to consider its effects. In 'Happy Accidents' the damaged photographs of Robert Capa provide the means to evoke the horror of war, not so much by the images they depict but by the flaws on them that suggest the effects of bullets and bomb blasts – the 'blister' of the silver, the 'melt' of the emulsion, with their 'fires' that 'caught/and smoked'.

The reader is invited not to apportion blame for violence, but to consider its effects

Probably the most political poem that deals with conflict is 'Drinking with Hitler', which, unlike the others mentioned above, focuses on a leader in a conflict. It is also the poem that deals with the most recent conflict, the civil unrest in Zimbabwe. While the focus is on Hunzvi's falseness and his abuse of power, it also provides images of the torture to which he was said to have subjected his opponents.

Love

The collection explores several aspects of love, from the solid, shared life forged by the speaker's parents in 'Inheritance' and the candour of self-revelation in 'Last Act' to the immature and exploitative relationships in 'Joseph Jones' and 'Drinking with Hitler'. Many of the love poems deal with moments of separation, or have a sense of detachment. Even in possibly the most joyful of the love poems, 'Song', much of the narrative deals with the consequences of separation after the female magpie has been trapped.

The precariousness of love is seen in poems that suggest break-up and reconciliation, which seem to be constants in love, whatever the setting. 'Winter Swans' depicts such a situation taking place in the countryside, where the folding of a bird's wings 'after flight' is like the interlocking of lovers' fingers after a falling-out. 'Show' evokes a similar situation in a sophisticated urban setting as the lovers attend a fashion show and stay in a city hotel. Here the imagery is more artificial, as make-up and jewellery enhance the woman's beauty, helping to make the male speaker fall in love anew.

Physical acts of love are depicted in urban and rural contexts

Despite the latter poem carrying a suggestion that the love presented is in some ways artificial, Sheers does not show love in the country as being true and love in the city as being false. Physical acts of love are depicted in urban and rural contexts and in both there is a sense of loss. For example, in 'Landmark' the countryside does not just evoke pastoral imagery: the lovers also see 'a long-dead sheep', evidence of the wider world in 'the telephone wires', and the mark in the grass where they had lain together is depicted as a 'sarcophagus … and complete without them'.

There is often distance between the male figure in the love poems and his lover. Many of the experiences are communicated in retrospect and have an elegiac tone, or a subtext of disappointment. 'Valentine', for example, recounts a trip to Paris, and concludes with an image of togetherness, but some readers might find this outweighed by the two images that preceded it, which both implied apartness. While the loose sonnet 'Marking Time' communicates an experience of urgent lust, it does so with the sense that love will fade like the 'mark upon' the loved one's back. The mark that might have been a badge of their love becomes seen as a 'brand-burn', a 'disturbance' and a 'scar'.

Many of the urban love poems present ambiguous experiences from distanced perspectives, which come in part from the stylised manner in which they are written. For example, 'Four Movements in the Scale of Two' uses the language of cinema, painting and writing to convey four moments in a relationship, and evokes an icy climax when the woman seems to announce the break-up; this is rendered in spare two-line stanzas that use cold imagery and a kind of slow motion pace. 'Night Windows' uses the language of painting and artificial lighting to render the experience of making love in a living room while the neighbours look on. In this poem it is not just the neighbours who are the

TASK

Remind yourself of the other love poems in the collection. Consider 'Marking Time', 'Show', 'Valentine', 'Winter Swans', 'Night Windows', 'Keyways' and 'Song'. To what extent do you agree with the view that Sheers' love poems are always marred by the distance between the speaker and the experiences he presents?

voyeurs: the speaker details only painterly or photographic fragments of his lover and, when the poem reaches its final stanza and the speaker's lover rises from him 'with a sigh', trailing her 'shadow' behind her, it seems as if a separation not a coupling has taken place.

Despite being one of the least ambiguous love poems, 'Keyways' also presents paradoxical aspects of love. As the speaker and his girlfriend stand in the queue at the locksmith's, he remembers the physical and spiritual closeness of the relationship that they are in the process of dissolving. As in other Sheers love poems, a tantalising sense of what might have been is palpable, especially in the questions near the climax of the poem when the speaker wonders: 'So when did the bolt slip? The blade break in the mouth?' Part of the poignant emotional power of such moments is that while, undeniably, they happen, it is nearly impossible to notice them approaching and, even in retrospect, it is difficult to pinpoint when they took place.

Gender

The poems might also be explored according to the ways in which they address masculinity or femininity. In addition to love poems that explore the beauty of women or the puzzling nature of relationships, there are those such as 'On Going' and 'Amazon' that demonstrate female bravery.

Masculinity is explored in a number of poems, from the uncomfortable recognition of brutality in men that we see in 'Hedge School', 'Late Spring', 'Drinking with Hitler' and 'The Fishmonger' to the strong but quiet masculinity in 'Grandfather', 'The Hill Fort', 'The Farrier' and 'Trees'. While there are rural poems of fathers and sons such as 'Farther' that suggest continuity and belonging, there is also the sense of lonely male grief in 'Y Gaer', as well as pathos in the lives of those who have slipped to the margins of society in 'The Singing Men'.

CRITICAL VIEW

'Sheers' love poems are most moving when he writes about love in the context of nature and the countryside.' Examine this view of *Skirrid Hill*.

Context

Some themes that Sheers himself sees in the collection include 'the ongoing dialogue between man and nature, the fraying of love' and 'questions of failed articulacy' (Sheers, 2008, p.32).

The poet's methods

Target your thinking

- Consider the different methods that Sheers uses in *Skirrid Hill*: which are the most important in each poem, and how are they used to shape meaning and to create effects? (**AO2**)
- As you consider methods and meaning, note uses of literary terms; how can you use literary terminology to help you to articulate your responses with more precision and concision? (**AO1**)
- How might your understanding of poetic methods help you to make connections with your comparative set text (if relevant to your exam board)? (**AO4**)
- In what ways can different close readings lead to alternative interpretations? (**AO5**)

This section is designed to offer you approaches to Assessment Objective 2 (Analyse ways in which meanings are shaped in literary texts). To address this effectively you need to respond to the poetic methods that Sheers uses in his poems. Note that the AO no longer names form, structure and language; this is a liberating invitation for you to concentrate on the poetic techniques that are most pertinent to the poems in question. Avoid simply naming techniques: comment on their effects and how they shape meaning. The following sub-sections remind you of some of the techniques that Sheers uses and their effects.

Form and genre

Rather than conforming to rigid patterns of stress and rhyme, most of Sheers' poems are written in free verse. Like many poems by writers such as Robert Frost and Edward Thomas, they follow the rhythms of speech. Read them aloud and you will follow their lines of thought and appreciate their musicality more easily. Despite being in free verse, the poems often follow stanzaic patterns and sometimes Sheers varies stanza length to create effects. For example, the single-line stanza at the end of 'The Equation' encourages the reader to marvel at the magic of the egg in the hand of the teacher who is also a farmer.

Sheers' favourite stanzaic form is the tercet, or three-line stanza. This encourages economy and is good for capturing an image or a thought. Poems that depend on more detailed narratives use longer stanzas. For example, 'Keyways' has five-line stanzas with a two-line stanza at the end to emphasise the conclusion that arises from the story. Quatrains are an excellent stanzaic form for storytelling and are used in narrative poems such as 'Liable to Floods' and 'Drinking with Hitler'. Sheers feels that the shapes of a poem on the page and the white space around it are important, and this can be seen in both longer and shorter stanzaic forms. For example, the insubstantial lives of 'The Singing Men' seem to suit their unrhymed two-line stanzas, while the tall block of text in 'Farther', which is reminiscent of the tall stanzas of Edward Thomas' 'The Mountain Chapel', seems to suit the climb up the Skirrid and the rock-solid relationship between father and son.

Sheers also makes use of standard forms, though these are often given a modern twist. For example, 'Marking Time' is a sonnet, which means that readers may come to it with the expectations of reading a love poem. Although the poem does not have a rigid metre or rhyme scheme, the subject matter of the poem does not disappoint, and Sheers also exploits the reader's understanding of the sonnet form to make intertextual play. A traditional sonnet often contains a volta – a turning point, where an idea takes a new direction or where there is a marked shift in tone. In Sheers' sonnet, he uses the word 'volte' to evoke a shift in the narrative as he describes the mark made by the woman's flesh rubbing on the carpet while they made love.

> Sheers makes use of standard forms, although these are often given a modern twist

Another traditional form is used in the four haiku that make up 'Calendar'. These poems are the most formally conventional in the collection as they fully meet the reader's expectations of the haiku form, both in terms of subject matter and style.

The poems in *Skirrid Hill* are lyric poems. If we think of sub-genres, Sheers might be said to use especially the love poem and the elegy. The last form is seen specifically in those poems that elegise his grandparents, 'The Wake' and 'On Going', but there is also a strongly elegiac feeling to some of the love poems, such as 'Keyways' and in 'Border Country', a poem that might be considered an elegy for lost youth.

Structure

It's worth paying attention to the ways in which the experience in a poem is sequenced. This might involve the ways images have been juxtaposed or how a narrative begins, develops and ends. For example, in 'Winter Swans' there is an organic development implied by the image of diving swans being followed by that of the couple holding hands, their fingers overlapping like the wings of a swan 'after flight'. This poem is also an example of Sheers finishing with a stanza of different length to the others. Here, as in other poems such as 'The Equation' or 'Amazon', the shorter stanza closes the poem on a climactic image that resonates with what went before. Sometimes poems recount an experience then finish on a shorter stanza that provides a closing thought and a kind of conclusion; this effect can be seen in poems such as 'Valentine', 'Keyways' and 'The Wake'.

'Y Gaer (*The Hill Fort*)' and 'The Hill Fort (*Y Gaer*)' make an interesting pair of poems. While they are similar in terms of narrative structure – each poem narrates an experience then offers a conclusion arising from that experience – in some ways they are opposing versions of the same story. There is a kind of mirroring effect, not just in the titles or in the way in which they face each other on opposite pages of the book, but also in the poems' styles. The first provides an outsider's perspective on the grief expressed on the hill; the second provides the insider's perspective on the happiness associated with the hill. The first is written in a spare style that is dense with imagery; in the second the language is looser and more colloquial.

The structure of the collection

Taking it further ▶

Why not compare 'Mametz Wood' to some of the poems that First World War poets wrote about the battle that took place there? 'A Dead Boche' by Robert Graves is a good starting point. A copy of the poem may be found at www. bartleby.com/120/19. html. Discussion of *In Parenthesis* by David Jones may be found at http:// tinyurl.com/3sdg7wp. Clips of Owen Sheers' documentary on *In Parenthesis* may be found at www.bbc.co.uk/ programmes/b07kt9pj.

The way in which the poems have been sequenced gives the collection coherence, even if this is not obvious at first. 'Mametz Wood', which describes the discovery of a mass grave from the First World War, seems an unusual opening poem for a book whose title is a place in Wales, but even this seemingly anomalous choice proves fitting. There are poems in the book's second half that relate to war, such as 'Happy Accidents' (which explores how we represent conflict by recounting a story from the career of the photographer, Robert Capa) and 'Liable to Floods' (which tells of how the plans of American soldiers were confounded by the Welsh landscape and weather). 'Mametz Wood' also has Welsh and poetic resonances, since it was here that the 38th (Welsh) Division of the British Army fought, suffering heavy losses in battles that have been widely written about by poets, including the Welsh writers David Jones and Wyn Griffith. The poem also relates to many of those that follow, since it engages with both loss and the landscape, and it adopts formal features such as tercets and free verse, which are typical of Sheers' style.

After 'Mametz Wood', the book's first half is personal: there is a sequence of 6 love poems, then 11 poems of family or growing up that draw on the poet's Welsh background. It is also worth noticing which poems are placed together. For example, 'The Equation', a poem about Sheers' maternal grandfather, who balanced work as a headteacher and a farmer, is accompanied by 'Late Spring', a poem inspired by the times when Sheers helped him castrate lambs. The most obvious pairing comes in the middle of the collection with 'Y Gaer (*The Hill Fort*)' and 'The Hill Fort (*Y Gaer*)' – poems that are formally similar to 'Mametz Wood' and which explore the intense feelings and lasting impact of a moment when lives are shaken by death. Given prominence by their central position, these poems chime with both the collection's title – with its sense of adopting a high vantage point – and its closing poem, 'Skirrid Fawr', which sees the landscape as numinous and enlightening.

After the rupture of this pair comes 'Intermission', whose title implies a break between two parts of a performance, which is appropriate for a poem that engages with the idea of a break in normal life caused by the darkness brought by a power cut. It also offers a kind of interval after the first half of the book. When we remember that the prefatory poem, 'Last Act', developed an extended metaphor of the poet as actor, this seems even more apt. Indeed the poem's slow pace and sense of a world slowed, stilled and simplified by the failure of what enables the frenetic pace of our lives is a welcome moment of light relief.

The second half of the collection seems less unified than the first, as the poet moves from his local environment to explore the wider world. Indeed as the collection progresses beyond its mid-point the first person pronoun recedes. Personal poems are still included, but these are distanced from the experiences that they present – even when the first person is adopted and the subject matter is as intimate as love. For example, the joyously sentimental 'Song', while written in the first person, is a self-consciously old-fashioned emotional song that engages with the universal rather than the personal. By contrast, the first person persona in 'Four Movements in the Scale of Two' adopts a modern, detached perspective – 'Cut to us, an overhead shot, early morning' – which, while moving in to finish with a close-up, leaves the reader not with a realistic description (such as the scar from carpet burn in 'Marking Time') but with a stylised, cinematic image that provides an **objective correlative** for the feelings of lovers who are breaking up:

> a glass
> dull-snapping in the hand
> beneath the washing water,
>
> that gives no sign it has done so
> until the slow smoke-signal of blood,
> uncurling from below.

There is a sinister beauty in these lines: the harsh stresses and plosives of the 'glass/dull-snapping' jolt the reader, and combine with the image of the 'slow smoke-signal' and the sibilance that accompanies the cut and trail of blood to lend the poem's conclusion a disturbing feel that is akin to a shock from a thriller or horror film.

As we saw earlier, it is typical for a Sheers poem to come to a resonant conclusion; others close with a significant thought, and several raise questions that send the reader back to what went before. The latter is the case with the final poem, 'Skirrid Fawr', whose last lines shine a new light on the earlier lines, casting shadows on assumptions that landscape offers solace, healing and all 'the answers'.

The light that 'Skirrid Fawr' shines is also cast back over the whole collection. The last two lines – 'Her weight, the unspoken words/of an unlearned tongue' – might remind us of the masculine reticence in poems from the first part of the collection such as 'Farther' and 'Trees' in which love, the continuance of traditions and a sense of belonging are evoked, as well as the sense of impeded fluency of speech that is conveyed in 'Last Act' and 'Inheritance'. This idea

objective correlative the technique of using something external, such as a concrete description, an image or a symbol, to objectify and evoke an emotion.

develops in the last line of 'Skirrid Fawr': from words to language itself as we are presented with the paradoxical notion of the speaker being at one with the landscape, yet apart from it (which seems entirely apt for a collection that has shown the poet being both a citizen of Wales and a citizen of the world). The 'unlearned tongue' reminds us of the Welsh language, perhaps conveying the poet's desire to be more fluent in that tongue as well as its importance to Welsh culture in general. The way in which the 'tongue' has been 'unlearned' might also suggest that aspects of Welsh culture have been forgotten and that this loss is a 'weight' on the country. In addition, the collection's final thought and final word enhance its coherence, since they remind us of the final image in the collection's first poem: those other, literal tongues that were silenced in Mametz Wood; those allied soldiers whose jaws were open:

> As if the notes they had sung
> have only now, with this unearthing,
> slipped from their absent tongues.

Language

The language in which Sheers' poems are written is often conversational, making the reader feel that the speaker is recounting an experience in a fluent, natural and immediate way. For example, 'Happy Accidents' begins as if the speaker is mid-conversation with the addressee: 'And Robert Capa, how was he to know?'

Many of the poems use real speech

Many of the poems use real speech. For example, 'The Hill Fort' uses direct speech to give the bereaved man a voice, and the language that Sheers gives him – 'from here in this view, 9, 19 or 90 years/are much the same' – is both poetic and authentic. In 'Liable to Floods' there is an entertaining contrast between the reticent warning of the Welsh farmer and the brash response of the American major. Speech is also used to create drama and atmosphere, for example in the kitchen of 'Service', in the 'Check!' that causes the 'submarine' to 'dive'.

While the reader's attention is rarely jolted by self-conscious poetic devices, Sheers does make use of various literary effects; although, as in the alliteration of '9, 19 or 90' in the example above, they tend to arise naturally from the subject matter of the poem. Rhyme is often used to link ideas, to make ideas stand out or to provide a resonant finish. For example, in 'Flag' the poignancy of Welsh identity in crisis is made more emphatic by the use of balanced rhythm and rhyme at the end of the poem, when 'red white and green' chimes with 'what might have been'.

Possibly the most significant literary feature used by Sheers is metaphor. From the gruesome 'dance-macabre' of the singing skeletons in 'Mametz Wood' to the 'tattered flags' of the 'loving scar' in 'Marking Time' to the 'great ship' in 'The Wake', metaphors seem to arise naturally from their subjects but also help Sheers evoke the essence of the experience. Aside from such concrete descriptive usages, Sheers uses metaphor in more enigmatic ways. For example, the reader must ponder the actual words said in the '*Eastern Promise*' section of 'Four Movements in the Scale of Two', where the final image of the 'blood,/ uncurling from below' is part of an extended metaphor of a glass cracking. This expresses an undefined event, which is itself a metaphor: 'what gave'.

Another, more ambiguous, device used is symbolism. For example, in 'Border Country' the 'buzzards' that were part of the boys' childhood experiences in the car graveyard return at the end of the poem, perhaps adding an uncanny feeling of the inescapable nature of the past and offering a more distanced perspective on the boys' experience, as well as perhaps suggesting the death of childhood and the death of a part of the boy whose father committed suicide.

Some elements of language and imagery recur in the collection. Natural motifs such as birds, horses and water are prevalent, as is language drawn from medicine, which can be seen in poems such as 'The Wake', 'Flag' and 'Calendar'. Magic is often evoked, both to show fascination in poems concerned with country lore such as 'The Equation' and 'The Farrier' and to draw attention to beauty and artifice in more metropolitan poems such as 'Show' and 'Shadow Man'. Writing provides self-referential language as well as descriptive imagery in many poems such as 'Marking Time', 'Swallows' and 'Border Country'. Other art forms influence Sheers' language too. For example, 'Four Movements in the Scale of Two' and 'Night Windows' both use painting and cinema, while 'Farther', 'Happy Accidents' and 'Shadow Man' use photography.

Build critical skills

Sheers has written that 'the intention of a poem is often to make the abstract world of thought and feeling concrete' (Sheers, 2009, p. xviii). To what extent do you think this is true of Sheers' use of metaphor? Cite examples of relevant metaphors and the thoughts or feelings that are evoked in each case.

Writing provides self-referential language as well as descriptive imagery in many poems

Contexts

Target your thinking

- How does contextual material help you to deepen your understanding of the poems? (**AO1**)
- In what ways can you apply contextual readings or critical approaches to the poems? (**AO3**)
- How does contextual understanding help you to make connections? (**AO4**)
- In what ways might your understanding of contexts lead you to consider alternative interpretations? (**AO5**)

Biography

Owen Sheers began writing as a poet, but has since branched out into various genres, including film, theatre and novel writing. He has presented arts programmes on radio and television and he wrote the script for the award-winning passion play staged in various locations around Port Talbot at Easter in 2011.

He was born in Fiji, where his mother worked as a teacher and his father as a town planner with the Overseas Development Agency. The family returned to the UK when Owen was two. They moved first to Wales, then to London and then back to Wales again when Owen was nine. He was educated at King Henry VIII comprehensive in Abergavenny and at New College, Oxford, where he read English; he later graduated with an MA from the University of East Anglia, where he was taught by Andrew Motion.

His first writing prize came at the age of ten, when he won the Abergavenny Agricultural Show Poetry Prize. It was the first of many successes, which include winning an Eric Gregory Award, a *Vogue* Young Writer's Award, being shortlisted for the Forward Prize for Best First Collection and the Welsh Book of the Year for *The Blue Book* (2000). His prose work, *The Dust Diaries* (2004), was short-listed for the Ondaatje Prize and won the Welsh Book of the Year. *Skirrid Hill* (2005) won the Somerset Maugham Award. His play about injured soldiers from Afghanistan, *The Two Worlds of Charlie F* (2012), won the Amnesty International Freedom of Expression Award at the Edinburgh Fringe.

His first novel, *Resistance* (2007), won the Hospital Club Creative Award and was shortlisted for the Writer's Guild Best Book Award. It has been made into a film starring Michael Sheen; Sheers co-wrote the screenplay. His 2015 novel *I Saw a Man* has won excellent reviews.

Despite his other successes, Sheers has continued his involvement with poetry. In 2009 the BBC screened his six-part series, *A Poet's Guide to Britain* (an anthology of the same name was published the same year). In 2010 Sheers' hour-long documentary entitled *Battlefield Poet: Keith Douglas* was broadcast on BBC4 to coincide with Remembrance Day and in 2016 the BBC broadcast his *The Greatest War Poem of World War One: David Jones's In Parenthesis*. Perhaps Sheers' most innovative use of verse has been in the creation of *Pink Mist* (2013), a five-part dramatic poem that explores the lives of three friends who joined the army together and served in Afghanistan. The winner of the Wales Book of the Year in 2014, it uses a mix of heightened dramatic verse and idiomatic speech to tell a gripping, poetic and resonant tale.

◀ Owen Sheers

War poet

Several of the poems in the collection explore aspects of war. The first considers the aftermath of a battle fought in Mametz Wood in the Somme region of northern France. The battle raged here on 7–12 July 1916, and 4,000 men from the 38th (Welsh) Division were killed or severely injured during the first three days. The writers Siegfried Sassoon and Robert Graves both fought in it, and Sheers' poem was inspired by a visit when, on the eighty-fifth anniversary of the battle, he went to make a short film about David Jones and Llewelyn Wyn Griffith, two Welsh poets who had written about fighting there. As well as responding to the direct experience of walking around the battlefield, Sheers was inspired by a news article, accompanied by a picture showing the mass grave:

There were 20 skeletons lying in it in various states of completeness, some still wearing rotten boots, others without. Each skeleton lay in its own position of death, but all of them were linked, arm in arm. It was a strange, touching, disturbing photograph

(Sheers, www.sheerpoetry.co.uk).

The First World War has continued to exert a fascination for Sheers. For example, he believes that some of the soldier poets who were not officers have been neglected and that one of these, the Welsh writer David Jones, wrote the best poem of the war. His *The Greatest Poem of World War One: David Jones's In Parenthesis* was broadcast by the BBC on 9 July 2016.

Sheers' first novel, *Resistance* (2007) explores the Second World War, imagining the consequences of failed D-Day landings and a successful German invasion of Britain. He also admires the Second World War poet Keith Douglas and wrote a play about him (*Unicorns, Almost*, staged in 2006) and made a BBC documentary (2010). Like 'Mametz Wood', Douglas' '*Vergissmeinnicht*' (a post-1900 poem on AQA's Love through the Ages paper) conveys a touching sense of waste – this time when a German gunner is discovered dead with a picture of his girlfriend near his body. Sheers' reference to the 'boots that outlasted' the dead soldiers is reminiscent of Douglas' German soldier's equipment which 'is hard and good while he's decayed'. An essay on Douglas by Sheers appeared in the *Guardian* and can be found at www.theguardian.com/stage/2005/may/28/theatre1.

Some of Sheers' most moving recent work has explored contemporary wars. *The Two Worlds of Charlie F.* (2012) is an innovative play that tells the stories of soldiers who were wounded – in some cases, losing legs – in Afghanistan. The script was developed through workshops with the soldiers themselves, several of whom act in performances of the play. *Pink Mist* was named as one of the *Independent*'s 50 Best Winter Reads in 2013 and the paper went so far as to call Sheers 'the war poet of our generation'. This work grew out of Sheers' research for *The Two Worlds of Charlie F.* and it explores the thoughts and experiences of three young soldiers who served in Afghanistan, this time through the medium of verse. Like *The Two Worlds of Charlie F.*, this verse-drama captures the soldiers' voices authentically. But, as well as being colloquial and idiomatic, Sheers' language is poetic – it even uses rhyming couplets. *Pink Mist* has been broadcast by BBC Radio 4 and versions have been staged in London and Bristol. Why, you might ask, does war seem to be such a preoccupation in Sheers' work? The answer has at least two parts. First, Sheers has spoken in interviews of the need for writers to keep on telling stories of war so long as people persist in using violence as a means to solve their problems. And, secondly, major conflicts have run parallel with his writing life. Indeed some of the boys that Sheers knew at school began their army careers at sixteen years old.

Literary contexts

The literary influences on Sheers have been many and various, as you might expect from a graduate in English from Oxford and in creative writing from the University of East Anglia (where he was taught by the former Poet Laureate, Andrew Motion). While it may not be helpful to place him a poetic tradition or to categorise *Skirrid Hill* as belonging to a particular poetic school, it is interesting to consider some of the writers who have impressed Sheers, or who have perhaps influenced particular poems. You might like to research those poets that Sheers admires and consider what it is he admires about them; watching or listening to the programmes he has written is a good starting point. In particular, it's worth hearing what he has to say about David Jones and Keith Douglas, poets who wrote about the First and Second World War respectively. You can also find out how Sheers relates to poets such as Wordsworth, Matthew Arnold and Louis MacNeice by watching his DVD, *A Poet's Guide to Britain*.

More obviously Welsh influences include Dannie Abse (1923–2014), whose work displays what Sheers calls 'a humanistic generosity' but 'needling scrutiny' about the darker side of life (Sheers, 2015, whyilovethisbook.com) and R. S. Thomas (1913–2000), who was one of the most highly regarded Welsh poets of the last century. 'Inheritance' is written '*After R. S. Thomas*' and perhaps in this poem (like 'The Farrier') Sheers is suggesting the importance of Welshness as part of his own identity. Like Thomas, Sheers grew up an English speaker and had a strong sense of both the Welsh and English aspects to his identity. While Thomas was conscious of being Anglo-Welsh, Sheers, it seems – particularly when we consider that he was born in Fiji and has travelled widely (as is suggested by several of the poems in the latter half of the collection) – is not just a citizen of Wales or England, but a citizen of the world. Again like Thomas, Sheers has had to balance some aspects of Welsh background against the need to be accessible to his non-Welsh audience, for example, by making the collection's title *Skirrid Hill* – to locals, the mountain is simply the Skirrid.

Another important literary precursor is Edward Thomas. Like Sheers and R. S. Thomas, he had an interesting background that combines aspects of Welshness and Englishness. While born in London, his parents were Welsh. He is acclaimed for the easy conversational rhythms of many of his poems and his depictions of the countryside. Sheers' thoughts about landscape might remind us of Thomas. Indeed he selected five of Thomas' poems for his *Poet's Guide to Britain* (2009). One is 'The Mountain Chapel', which is written in tall stanzas – two of 16 lines and one of 10 – and gives a voice to the wind, which says:

'Tis but a moment since man's birth,

And in another moment more

Man lives in earth

For ever; but I am the same

Now, and shall be, even as I was

Before he came:

Till there is nothing I shall be.'

Like Thomas' poem, albeit in a less direct way, poems by Sheers such as 'Farther' and 'Trees' convey a comforting sense that the landscape which shaped people will endure long after they are gone.

The Welsh landscape

Sheers has acknowledged the influence of the landscape on his work. As he notes in the introduction to his *A Poet's Guide to Britain*, 'I fell in love with the experience of the landscape, with how the hills and coasts of South Wales could alter my thoughts and feelings, long before I fell for poetry' (Owen Sheers, *A Poet's Guide to Britain*, London: Penguin, 2009, p. xvii). He also quotes Heaney on how knowing a place comes in two opposite yet complementary ways: 'One is lived, illiterate and unconscious, the other learned, literate and conscious. In the literary sensibility, both are likely to co-exist in a conscious and unconscious tension' (Heaney, quoted by Sheers, 2009, p. xix). You might like to think about how such ideas might be borne out in poems such as 'The Hill Fort' and 'Y Gaer' and 'Skirrid Fawr'. Sheers has also spoken in interviews of the ways in which knowing a landscape is important to a writer. As well as having a personal sense of engagement with a place, there is a sense of a shared landscape that brings wider cultural connections. As with Seamus Heaney, a strong sense of place gives the writer a solid foundation from which to write as well as something to dig down into and explore.

It's worth researching some of the specific aspects of the landscape mentioned in *Skirrid Hill*. For example, you can discover that there are several legends surrounding the Skirrid. The one alluded to in 'Farther' is probably 'the legend that the mountain was rent asunder by the earthquake which happened at the crucifixion of the Saviour: hence it has obtained the appellation of *Holy Mount*, a name under which it is best known among the inhabitants of the county' (from an account of 1810). This is in keeping with the spiritual dimension which Sheers gives the landscape.

Socio-economic contexts

It is not only the spiritual side of Welsh life that Sheers presents in *Skirrid Hill*. Some poems respond to changes in Welsh culture and society that are far from comforting. For example, 'Border Country' hints at the discontent in rural communities. Depression among farmers was a particular concern in the 1990s and early 2000s, and, in 2001, a coroner linked the deaths of three farmers to pressures caused by epidemics affecting livestock, such as BSE and foot-and-mouth disease (http://news.bbc.co.uk/1/hi/wales/1388666.stm). In 2000, British farmers' incomes had dropped for the fifth year in succession, with those farming cereals being the worst hit by a drop of 25 per cent. Those in Wales were among the worst affected.

The decline in some Welsh towns is suggested by loutish behaviour in 'Joseph Jones' and the lack of purposeful work available in 'The Steelworks,'. The latter poem responds to real events in Ebbw Vale, where steel production stopped on 5 July 2002. The factory here had been founded in

1790, and until its closure, it was the biggest tinplate producer in Britain. It had been at the forefront of technological development in its conversion of iron to steel, but the closure of the works led to far-reaching consequences. Some workers had to relocate, or seek employment in new trades often for much lower wages. Many of those in jobs that serviced the steelworks found themselves unemployed. Some suffered from depression, alcoholism or family breakdown. The ill-effects of the closure were being felt when Sheers was writing *Skirrid Hill*, though in 2007 a regeneration project began and now the area is thriving (www.walesonline.co.uk/lifestyle/nostalgia/steeling-themselves-what-port-talbot-10811580).

National identity

Despite the above comments about the landscape and the importance of Wales, Sheers does not like the idea of his work being pigeon-holed. As he said in an interview for *The Poetry Archive*:

I've never been too fond of the idea of writers being limited by their borders – you know one of the reasons that I write, one of the reasons I love writing, is that it can go further than any border, any boundary so I tend to describe myself as a writer from Wales, rather than being a Welsh writer

(The Poetry Archive
http://www.poetryarchive.org/interview/
owen-sheers-interview)

This is even more understandable when we think of the range of creative work he has produced: Sheers is not only a poet, but also a playwright, a novelist, a presenter, a screenwriter, a librettist and so on.

Rather than identifying with a single place, Sheers' sense of identity is plural. This might be seen in the subtext of his poem 'Flag', which was written when Sheers returned to Wales after being away for 18 years and was taken aback by the proliferation of Welsh flags, which were being hung out to show support for devolution in Wales (the transfer of more powers from London to Cardiff). In September 1997, the Welsh voted, by 50.3 per cent to 49.7 per cent, for a separate legislative assembly for Wales.

While Sheers' work obviously presents a love of Wales and its landscape, it does not seem to advocate nationalism or an exclusive Welsh culture. As he told a journalist, 'Being Welsh is important, but I'm nervous of the idea of a writer being defined by their nationality' (*Jersey Evening Post*, 19 July 2015). In June 2016, Sheers signed a letter backing support for Britain to remain in the European Union. His sense of pluralism might also be seen in many of the poems in the collection's second part. It is also suggested by his having lived in cosmopolitan places like London and New York, and possibly by having been born in Fiji.

Context

At the age of 18, Sheers returned to Fiji to work for six months as a volunteer as well as to find the tree under which his umbilical cord had been buried. Listen to the interview with Sheers for *Private Passions*, http://www.bbc.co.uk/programmes/b06k9f26

Assessment Objectives and skills

> **AO1** Articulate informed, personal and creative responses to literary texts, using associated concepts and terminology, and coherent, accurate written expression.

To do well with AO1 you need to write fluently, structuring your essay carefully, guiding your reader clearly through your line of argument and using the sophisticated vocabulary, including critical terminology, which is appropriate to an A-level essay. You will need to use frequent embedded quotations to show detailed knowledge and demonstrate familiarity with the whole text. Your aim is to produce a well-written academic essay employing appropriate discourse markers to create the sense of a shaped argument.

> **AO2** Analyse ways in which meanings are shaped in literary texts.

Strong students do not work only on a lexical level, but write well on the generic and structural elements of the poems in *Skirrid Hill*, so it is useful to start by analysing those larger elements of narrative organisation before considering the poets' use of language. If 'form is meaning', what are the implications of this for each poem? Then again, to discuss language in detail you will need to quote from poems, analyse what you quote and use it to illuminate your argument. Since you will at times need to make points about generic and organisational features of the text much too long to quote in full, being able to reference closely and effectively is just as important as mastering the art of the embedded quotation. Practise writing in analytical sentences, comprising a brief quotation or close reference, a definition or description of the feature you intend to analyse, an explanation of how this feature has been used and an evaluation of its effects.

> **AO3** Demonstrate understanding of the significance and influence of the contexts in which literary texts are written and received.

To access AO3 you need to think about how contexts of production, reception, literature, culture, biography, geography, society, history, genre and intertextuality can affect texts. Place each poem at the heart of a web of contextual factors which you feel have had the most impact upon it; examiners want to see a sense of contextual alertness woven seamlessly into the fabric of your prose rather than a clumsy rehash of your history notes. Show you understand that literary works contain encoded representations of the cultural, moral, religious, racial and political values of the society from which they emerged, and that over time attitudes and ideas change until the views they reflect are no longer widely shared.

> **A04** Explore connections across literary texts.

If your examination requires you to compare and contrast one or more other texts with *Skirrid Hill* you must find specific points of comparison, rather than merely generalising. You will find it easier to make connections between texts (of any kind) if you balance them as you write; remember also that connections are not only about finding similarities – differences are just as interesting. Above all, consider how the comparison illuminates each text; some connections will be thematic, others generic or stylistic.

> **A05** Explore literary texts informed by different interpretations.

For this AO, you should refer to the opinions of critics and remain alert to aspects of the poems that are open to interpretation. Your job is to measure your own interpretation of the text against those of other readers. Try to convey an awareness of multiple readings as well as an understanding that (as Barthes suggested) a text's meaning is dependent as much upon what you bring to it as what the poet left there. Using modal verb phrases such as 'may be seen as', 'might be interpreted as' or 'could be represented as' shows you know that different readers interpret texts in different ways at different times. The key word here is plurality; there is no single meaning or one right answer. Relish getting your teeth into the views of published critics to push forward your own argument, but always keep in mind that meanings in poems are shifting and unstable as opposed to fixed and permanent.

Summary

Overall, the hallmarks of a successful A-level essay that hits all five AOs include the following:

- a clear introduction that orientates the reader and outlines your main argument;
- a coherent and conceptualised argument that relates to the question title;
- confident movement around the text rather than a relentless chronological trawl through it;
- apt and effective quotations or references adapted to make sense within the context of your own sentences;
- a range of effective points about Sheers' methods;
- a strong and personally engaged awareness of how a text can be interpreted by different readers and audiences in different ways at different times;
- a sense that you are prepared to take on a good range of critical and theoretical perspectives; and
- a conclusion that effectively summarises and consolidates your response and relates it back to your essay title.

Building Skills 1: Structuring your writing

This section focuses on responses to convey your ideas as clearly and effectively as possible: the 'how' of your writing as opposed to the 'what'. More often than not, if your knowledge and understanding of *Skirrid Hill* is sound, a disappointing mark or grade will be down to one of two common mistakes: misreading the question or failing to organise your response economically and effectively. In an examination you'll be lucky if you can demonstrate 5 per cent of what you know about *Skirrid Hill*; luckily, if it's the right 5 per cent, that's all you need to gain ful marks.

Understanding your examination

It's important to prepare for the type of response to *Skirrid Hill* that your exam board requires. If you're studying the text for AS with WJEC (Wales only), you answer two questions. One requires close comment on a single poem from *Skirrid Hill*. The other is comparative – you respond to a viewpoint and explore connections between poems from *Skirrid Hill* and *Field Work* by Seamus Heaney. For the Eduqas A level, you respond to a single question, which cites a viewpoint about the poetry of Sheers and Heaney. It requires you to make connections between poems from *Skirrid Hill* and *Field Work*. As with the comparative question for WJEC (Wales only), your response must cover four poems: two from each text. For the AQA A A-level, check with your teacher. Typically, for this specification, you'll study *Skirrid Hill* as a poetry set text and examine a viewpoint on the collection in Section A of the exam. (There is also the option to study the collection as a comparative set text and to compare poems from *Skirrid Hill* to your other comparative set text, chosen as part of the Modern Times option.) For all of the syllabuses mentioned above, you may take a clean, unannotated copy of the text into the examination room.

Open book

In an open book exam when you have a copy of *Skirrid Hill* beside you, there is little excuse for failing to quote relevantly, accurately and extensively. To gain a high mark, you must focus in detail on specific parts of the text. Remember, too, that you must not refer to any supporting material such as an introduction or notes contained within your edition of the text. If an examiner suspects that you have been lifting unacknowledged material from such a source, they will refer your paper to the examining body for possible malpractice.

Non-examined assessment (NEA)

Writing about *Skirrid Hill* within a non-examined assessment unit context poses a different set of challenges from an examination in that bungled quotations and disorientating arguments are liable to cost you much more dearly. Your essay must be wholly and consistently relevant to the title selected; there's no excuse for going off track if you and/or your teacher mapped out the parameters of your chosen topic in the first place.

Step 1: Planning and beginning: locate the debate

A common type of exam question invites you to open up a debate about the text by using various trigger words and phrases such as 'examine the view that …' or 'how far do you agree with this view?' When considering this type of question, the one thing you can be sure of is that exam questions never offer a view that makes no sense at all or is so blindingly obvious all anyone can do is agree with it. There will always be a genuine interpretation at stake. So, your introduction must address the terms of this debate and sketch out the outlines of how you intend to move the argument forward to orientate the reader. Since you need to know this before you start writing, you must plan before you write.

Undertaking a lively debate about some of the ways in which the Sheers poems have been and can be interpreted is the DNA of your essay. Of course, any good argument needs to be honest; to begin by writing 'Yes, I totally agree with this obviously true statement' suggests a fundamental misunderstanding of what studying literature is all about. The given views in examination questions are designed to open up critical conversations, not shut them down.

Plan your answer by collecting points for and against the given view. Aim to see a stated opinion as an interesting way of focusing on a key facet of *Skirrid Hill* or the poem under discussion.

Student A

This student is answering an A level examination question in the style of Eduqas, Unit 2, Section B: Poetry Comparison.

'At its core, poetry is personal.' In response to this view, explore connections between the ways in which Heaney and Sheers write about themselves and their country. Analyse at least two poems from each of your set texts in depth.

It is easy to agree that Heaney and Sheers write from personal experience, but it would be naïve to suggest their work is purely autobiographical. This essay focuses on two main aspects. First, both use the place they come from to explore wider issues. For example, both Sheers' 'Flag' and Heaney's 'The Toome Road' are less about personal interactions with their homelands and more about using these places to evoke identity struggles and chart shifting political landscapes. Secondly, the poets write about places to explore stories that are not theirs personally. While the bilingual place-name poems 'Y Gaer (*The Hill Fort*)' and 'The Hill Fort (*Y Gaer*)' might suggest fractured national identity, the poems use the named landscape to narrate a personal story of grief and fractured identity, but this narrative is not based on the poet's personal experience. Conversely, 'In Memoriam Francis Ledwidge' does use Heaney's personal experience and the landscape of the North West of his country as the impetus for retelling someone else's story — that of the Irish soldier poet — and to explore aspects of national identity.

To turn to the first aspect in more detail, 'Flag' and 'The Toome Road' both have titles that suggest concerns about their respective countries. Sheers' title, which denotes the emblem of a country or a sign of conquest, suggests his poem's concern with national identity around the time. In Sheers' poem, which was written around the time of the Welsh referendum (on the country having its own parliament with powers held previously by the British parliament) in 1997, the presentation of the flags throughout Wales is uncomplimentary. 'Wrapped up in itself' and making a 'Chinese burn of red white and green', the flag imagery suggests that Wales is narcissistic or tortured by its nationalism. Indeed, this is something that chimes with Sheers' own political views. Despite journalists wanting to view him as a Welsh poet, he has said that he's 'never been too fond of the idea of writers being limited by their borders' and, more recently, has campaigned against Britain leaving the European Union. So it is unsurprising that his poem about national identity presents overt shows of nationalism as being unattractive. For example, in its final tercet, the flag is presented metaphorically as a 'tourniquet' or 'bandage' that mitigates the effects of a 'wound' and keeps in check 'the dreams of what might have been'. Sheers binds the connected ideas through rhyme: an internal half-rhyme links 'green' to 'dreams' and envelope rhyme connects 'red white and green' to 'what might have been'. The poem concludes with a resounding sense of failed promise.

While Sheers' poem can, therefore, be read as a criticism of Welsh nationalism in a vote to decide on a partial break with Britain, Heaney's might be read as a personal assertion of Irish nationalism in the face of a political situation that forces Northern Ireland into a closer union with Britain. And while Sheers' poem is overtly ideas-driven, Heaney's is driven by a first person narrative depicting a farmer witnessing the arrival of troops down county roads early one morning. His opening descriptions draw the reader into his world, appealing to both eyes and ears. The soldiers stand up in turrets of armoured cars that are 'camouflaged with broken alder branches'. The speaker's beloved countryside is literally being 'broken' and the aural imagery of the 'powerful tyres warbling along' sounds both ominous (with its humming sound) and uncanny as it takes the pleasing sound of birdsong and perverts this into the noise of the approach of an occupying force.

Examiner's commentary

This student:

- opens with a strong introductory paragraph: it engages fully with the terms of the question, providing a focused response and signposting the main areas that the essay is going to cover

- uses discourse markers to help guide the reader; as well as using sequences such as 'first' and 'secondly', the use of 'therefore' in the middle of the first sentence of the third paragraph helps the reader to follow the developing argument

- argues forcefully, but offers alternative readings and, where appropriate, expresses points tentatively

- adopts an analytical style, using well-chosen quotations and references fluently

- makes strong connections between the work of the two poets, developing ideas by comparison and contrast.

If the rest of the essay reached this level of performance, it is likely the student would achieve a notional grade A.

Step 2: Developing and linking: go with the flow

An essay is a very specific type of formal writing requiring an appropriate discourse structure. In the main body of your writing, you need to thread your developing argument through each paragraph consistently and logically, referring back to the terms established by the question itself, rephrasing and reframing as you go. It can be challenging to sustain the flow of your essay and keep firmly on track, but here are some techniques to help you:

- Ensure your essay doesn't disintegrate into a series of disconnected blobs by creating a stable bridge between one paragraph and the next.

◥ Use discourse markers – linking words and phrases like 'on the other hand', 'however', 'although' and 'moreover' – to hold the individual paragraphs of your essay together and signpost the connections between different sections of your overarching argument.

◥ Having set out an idea in Paragraph A, in Paragraph B you might need to then back this up by providing a further example; if so, signal this to your reader with a phrase such as '**Moreover** this idea is developed in the next two stanzas …'

◥ To change direction and challenge an idea begun in Paragraph A by acknowledging that it is open to interpretation, you could begin Paragraph B with something like '**On the other hand**, this view of the text could be challenged by a feminist critic …'

◥ Another typical paragraph-to-paragraph link is when you want to show that the original idea doesn't give the full picture. Here you could modify your original point with something like '**Although** it is possible to see the poem as being primarily about the desire for an affair, the potential love in the poem might be an allegorical representation of poetry …'

Student B

This student is answering an AS examination question in the style of WJEC Unit 2, Section A: Critical Analysis.

Re-read 'Border Country'. Explore the ways in which Sheers creates setting and atmosphere in this poem.

Furthermore, if we look back at the first stanza, we notice that it creates atmosphere in intriguing ways. The setting in the present tense is an open space; the 'car quarry' is no longer there. The only traces of the place where he played with abandoned cars as a boy are the 'raised earth' and the 'trees'. While 'trees' might suggest pastoral contentment, the 'car quarry' might be seen as an intrusion of industry into the natural world. Natural materials are usually extracted from a quarry, yet the quarry that is the setting of the childhood memories in the poem is a place where old cars were dumped. Similarly, there is a jarring blend of the natural and the industrial in the 'motorway pile-up in the corner of the field'. There is something sudden, violent and unexpected about a motorway accident, which perhaps foreshadows the sudden, violent and unexpected action of a farmer who shot himself in his own cornfield. It also links to the later metaphor to do with his son: the poem's whole atmosphere shifts at the point when 'life put on the brakes' and pitched him 'without notice,/through the windscreen of [his] youth'. Like a victim of a car crash, the boy's life changed suddenly, painfully and for the worse in an instant.

In addition, Sheers unsettles the reader subtly through his use of a semantic field of death. The raised earth is 'like the hummock of a grave'; the trees resemble 'a headstone', with leaves making 'epitaphs'; the site of the car quarry is like both 'an elephant's graveyard' and 'a motorway pile-up'. On first reading, each deathly detail might not strike the reader, but, cumulatively, they create an unsettling atmosphere and, on rereading, their proleptic function becomes clear as they foreshadow the death that is at the heart of the poem. Despite being only revealed in the fourth stanza, the effects of this death are suggested throughout the poem: from image of the lost boy in the final line to the sense of emptiness in the first.

Examiner's commentary

This student:

▼ uses discourse markers, such as 'furthermore', 'similarly' and 'in addition', to aid the coherence of the argument and make its development clear to the reader

▼ uses a flexible critical vocabulary – terms like 'proleptic', 'pastoral' and 'cumulatively' help the student write analytically and with precision

▼ keeps the answer relevant, referring to the exact words in the question – 'setting' and 'atmosphere' – confidently

▼ demonstrates detailed understanding of the poem and its ideas; note, for example, the flexible way in which the student selects material from throughout the text with ease

▼ analyses pertinent poetic methods, particularly language and narrative structure.

If the rest if the essay reached this level of performance, it is likely the student would achieve a notional grade A.

Step 3: Concluding: seal the deal

As you bring your writing to a close, you need to capture and clarify your response to the given view and make a relatively swift and elegant exit. Keep your final paragraph short. Now is not the time to introduce new points – but equally, don't just reword everything you have already just said. Neat potential closers include:

▼ looping the last paragraph back to something you mentioned in your introduction to suggest that you have now said all you have to say on the subject

▼ reflecting on your key points in order to reach a balanced overview

▼ ending with a punchy quotation that leaves the reader thinking

▼ discussing the contextual implications of the topic you have debated

▼ reversing expectations to end on an interesting alternative view

▼ stating why you think the main theme, concern or idea under discussion is so central to the text

▼ mentioning how different readers over time might have responded to the topic you have been debating.

Student C

This student is concluding an A level examination question in the style of Eduqas, Unit 2, Section B: Poetry Comparison.

'For both poets, the countryside is primarily a source of comfort and pleasure.' In response to this view, explore connections between the ways in which Heaney and Sheers write about the countryside. Analyse at least two poems from each of your set texts in depth.

Both poets, therefore, make use of simple narratives of life in the country, but the issues that they address are much more complex. The countryside is the backdrop for change. As you can see in 'Late Spring', life in the country does not just involve watching fluffy little lambs gambolling about in the fields, but it also involves castrating them! In addition, the poem is also about the change from boyhood to adolescence and it suggests the pains of growing up. Yet while Sheers and Heaney show the negative side of country life, it is Heaney who makes you think more and makes you sad more. His story of the badgers is scary and makes you wonder about the IRA. All in all, I agree with the quotation, but only to a degree.

Examiner's commentary

This student:

▼ demonstrates competent understanding, with some comment on the complexities of the question

▼ uses language in a sometimes straightforward way, for example, words like 'scary' and 'sad' are overly simple, the exclamatory sentence perhaps strikes the wrong tone and the final sentence seems overly brisk

▼ introduces what appears to be a fresh example in the final paragraph (involving 'Late Spring'), which is something that should be avoided in conclusions

▼ does compare competently.

If the rest of the essay reached this level of performance, it is likely the student would achieve a notional grade C.

Building Skills 2: Analysing texts in detail

Having worked through the previous Building Skills section on structuring your writing, this section contains a whole student response to a question on *Skirrid Hill.* This enables you to assess the extent to which the student has demonstrated their writing skills and mastery of the Assessment Objectives, and provides you with an index by which to measure your own skills. A commentary is provided to help you identify what is being done well.

Student D

This student is answering a question in the style of AQA Specification A for Paper 2B: Modern Times (Section A: Poetry Set Text)

'In *Skirrid Hill* love is presented as either mysterious or disappointing.'
Examine this view of the collection.

The quoted statement is perhaps too sweeping to be taken seriously. Of course there are some love poems in which lovers are mysterious and in which love disappoints, but that is by no means true of them all.

'Song' could be used to refute the statement. Here the speaker sings a song of love, wooing his lover by narrating the story of what he would do if they were magpies and she were caught in a trap. The sense of the poem as a traditional song, its non-specific title and its subject matter all lend the poem a timeless feel, as if the love evoked has a universality that applies to many people from many places. In addition, the sub-genre of song might suggest the poem is written in the tradition of lyrics that have been passed, by word of mouth, from generation to generation. The speaker and his lover add to this quality since they are unnamed. Rather than being specific people from a specific place or time they are archetypal lovers. These lovers are far from mysterious and their love is in no sense disappointing. In a gentle, yet confident, tone the speaker recounts exactly what he would do to help his trapped love: he would 'spread my wings in the rain/and fan you with my feathers in the sun'. Such simple images of love and protection communicate the devotion that extends whatever the weather or circumstances and the use of 'the rain' and 'the sun' places their love in a wholesome, natural context.

Rather than communicating disappointment, the poem suggests that love will bring satisfaction. In the final three stanzas the chronology expands from times of the day ('night' and 'morning') to seasons of the year. The final sentence is fittingly set during 'Spring', which adds to feelings of rebirth, and the reader shares in the satisfying message that patient and true love will triumph over adversity. The poem culminates in a joyous image of love reunited. Disrupting the normal stanzaic pattern of tercets, Sheers uses a quatrain to add weight to the final stanza and its sense of love setting the two birds free, as the speaker opens the cage and stands 'waiting/to help you try your wings again'. Imagery of birds' wings also suggest hope in 'Winter Swans', where the usual stanzaic form of tercets contracts at the close into a two-line stanza that zooms in on the lovers' hands as they come together 'like a pair of wings settling after flight'. Perhaps the 'flight' suggests that there were earlier difficulties in the relationship, but even so, the poem suggests satisfaction rather than disappointment — especially since the swans, which the addressee says 'mate for life', have connotations of beauty, majesty and fidelity.

It might be argued, however, that there is a sense of mystery around the woman, or the nature of the relationship, in this poem. In the second stanza, the lovers walk 'silent and apart' until they see the swans, and the discomfort in their relationship is also conveyed through natural imagery, such as the 'waterlogged earth/gulping for breath at our feet'. Such images, and the ugly-sounding use of onomatopoeia (with the word 'gulping'), might suggest that their relationship is at its last gasp, before the narrative delivers a welcome surprise with the beauty and unity of the swan imagery and the togetherness that it suggests.

There is a similar narrative trajectory from uncertainty to satisfaction in 'Show', another poem that communicates the mystery of a lover. Yet here the mystery seems part of the attraction. In contrast with the purity and universality of 'Song', this poem is set in specific and contemporary locations, a fashion show and a hotel, but the mystery is in the age-old crafts of make-up and body adornment. In the poem's second part a sundering is repaired as, aided by the mysteries of the 'mascara brush', 'the dress' and 'jewellery', the loved one leaves the speaker 'surrendered'. Mystery, in the sense of arcane lore, seems appropriate here, but this need not be considered as pejorative. As well as conferring power over the lover, her mysterious ability to transform herself and not be fully known is perhaps what keeps the love between she and the speaker alive.

While it would be untrue to suggest that the poem's conclusion delivers any sense of disappointment for the speaker, we might argue that the reader, if he or she chooses to read from an oppositional stance, could be disappointed. In this way, the reader might see the poem as dramatising the falseness of a late capitalist society and its emphasis on the surface of things. The first part of the poem presents the world of fashion — with its 'crocodile pit of cameras/flashing their teeth for more' — as predatory and eager to consume the things it loves. Perhaps Sheers' own biography might lend credence to such a view as he has experience of the fashion world through his winning a *Vogue* young writer's talent contest in 1999. The photographers might be symbolic of this showy culture and their insatiability might point to capitalism's paradoxical encouragement of desire — a desire whose satisfaction is endlessly deferred. Considered in this way, the more personal second part of the poem also disappoints, since the speaker's critical faculties have been beaten by his response to beauty — a beauty which is purely superficial. Indeed the speaker has been transformed into a voyeur who does not see the whole of his lover, but only artful fragments such as the jewellery, which resembles 'early stars against the dusk of [her] skin'. Accordingly, this might seem to be a superficial kind of love: the final stanza with its 'artful hocus-pocus' points to a cheap trick, which is reinforced in the final line (with which it rhymes) as the speaker perceives the room to be 'out of focus'. It is fitting that this poem of surfaces ends with an image inspired by a simple camera effect. Indeed, that final stanza might send us back to the title of the poem; we might decide that the 'Show', which we at first took to be a display or an entertainment, has metamorphosed into something marked by falsehood, something merely for 'Show'.

Another poem that could be used to substantiate the argument for Sheers' love poems presenting readers with mysterious lovers and disappointment in love is 'Four Movements in the Scale of Two'. Here the poet casts a critical eye over four stages in a relationship. He uses the language of art — writing, music, cinema and painting — to render the relationship and by so doing creates a distance from the experience of love that is antithetical to the simplicity of 'Song'. Despite the first section, 'Pages', being seemingly hopeful — the relationship is 'an open book/with blank pages' — there is mystery as the speaker is simultaneously both subject and observer: 'Cut to us, an overhead shot'. This disconcerting narrative stance, in which the poet is not just rendering experience but analysing it, certainly casts the loved one in a mysterious light. As in 'Show' there is a sense of fragments rather than of a whole person. The climax of the poem might be seen to arrive in section III when the loved one's words drop to her lover 'like the shock of new ice in old water'. This thermal image with its juxtaposed opposites and evocation of the sound as the ice hits the water — aided by the half-rhyme on 'like' and 'cracked' — is both arresting and mysterious. We are not told her words, but we might assume that they tell him she does not want their relationship to continue.

Disappointment is conveyed as much by the elegiac tone of the final section as by the pain and shock of the image of the broken glass. It is fitting that in such matters where the reasons for splitting up are not always perceptible by logic — even though those involved might like to subject them to endless analysis — Sheers finds an apt image that conveys both mystery and disappointment. The broken relationship is a source of mystery to both lovers as they are left 'puzzling over what gave'. The enigma of the love is encapsulated by the use of 'gave': a word that usually means 'presented', but here means 'broke'; something that is usually to do with giving, here, paradoxically, refers to something that has been taken away. The broken glass/broken relationship metaphor extends, conveying not only the mysterious hidden quality of the broken love (in the sense of it being buried in the 'washing water' and 'dull-snapping') but also the gathering pain and horror as evoked by the 'slow smoke-signal of blood' — an image that perhaps foreshadows future pain.

To a large degree, then, the quotation could be seen to be right, but only in some ways. It would be wrong to suggest that lovers in Sheers are always mysterious and love always disappointing, and the levels of mystery and disappointment are different in every love poem. Furthermore 'mystery' need not be taken in a pejorative sense. Like the woman in 'Show', those in 'Night Windows', 'Valentine' and 'Marking Time' might be seen to be mysterious to some degree, but it might be argued that this quality is what makes them attractive to the speaker or intriguing to the reader. As regards love being disappointing, I think that this is a little too strong. While many of the love poems do have a mood of dissatisfaction, this is to do with the reflective stance of the speaker, and more often than not, the poems could be seen as ending on a note that is closer to satisfaction; for example, the scar which might be seen as a symbol of love at the end of 'Marking Time' or the image of the two lovers 'holding each other on the hotel bed' in 'Valentine'. Perhaps the poem that creates the most overt sense of disappointment is 'Keyways', which is set at a locksmith's while a couple prepare to go their separate ways. Yet, despite ending on a note of disappointment, at its centre this poem reflects on the satisfaction of the lovers' earlier closeness: when they listened to Handel's *Messiah* in a chapel and their breaths were 'rising and falling in unison ... like a pair of Siamese twins sharing one lung'. This quasi-holy image of togetherness might be seen to represent a spiritual union, which is just as much a part of the relationship as the eventual break-up.

Perhaps Sheers is saying that mystery and disappointment are inevitable parts of human love, but so too are the happier experiences such as physical and spiritual togetherness. Whatever hardships love might bring, he seems to imply that its joys make it worth preserving. In the words of 'Song', which is perhaps his most straightforward and optimistic love poem, 'love is all there is to save'.

Examiner's commentary

- ◥ **AO1:** Relevant understanding of Sheers' poetry is conveyed with confidence and the answer is structured clearly and logically. A flexible literary vocabulary allows the student to analyse with precision and quotations are integrated seamlessly into the fabric of the prose.

- ◥ **AO2:** The analysis is assured, with pertinent points being made on form and structure as well as language. For instance, the generic qualities of 'Song' are explored and the central and closing images in 'Keyways' are considered.

- ◥ **AO3:** The student uses contextual understanding of capitalism and fashion as well as biographical references to Sheers to inform the argument. The biographical details are handled quite sensitively and the answer moves from text to context and back to text fluently without digressing.

- ◥ **AO4:** Connections between the poems are made with confidence and the argument is focused on the terms of the question, which are considered in detail. For example, the answer considers several interpretations of 'mystery' and makes distinctions between feelings of 'dissatisfaction' and 'disappointment'. The candidate makes good use of the question's key words and engages in debate throughout, beginning by countering the viewpoint, then moving to consider ways in which it has validity. The final paragraphs take a broader perspective, providing some overview of the collection, and the implications of some of the earlier analysis are explored.

- ◥ **AO5:** Perceptive and confident engagement with the view throughout, with assured use of the key words.

It is likely the student would achieve a notional grade A.

Taking it further

Websites

www.owensheers.co.uk Owen Sheers' own website is the best place to find out more about him and the full range of his writing. There are useful subsections, as well as links to other relevant sites.

www.poetryarchive.org The Poetry Archive entry for Owen Sheers; search on 'Poets' then 'Sheers'. This useful resource includes recordings of some poems, an interview and further details about Sheers.

www.bbc.co.uk/programmes/b06k9f26 Owen Sheers is the guest on this edition of the Radio 3 programme, *Private Passions*, first broadcast on 25 October 2015. As well as discussing his taste in classical music, Sheers offers thoughts on subjects ranging from Welshness to warfare.

Selected works by Sheers

Sheers, O. (2015) *I Saw a Man*, Faber. Sheers' latest novel is a gripping thriller that has moments of poetic grace.

—— (2013) *Pink Mist*, Faber. A recording of this award-winning verse drama that combines idiomatic speech and rhyming couplets with devastating effects can be downloaded via Owen's website.

—— (2012) *The Two Worlds of Charlie F.*, Faber. Sheers' play about injured veterans of Afghanistan is a moving theatrical experience.

—— (2009) *A Poet's Guide to Britain*, Penguin. The introduction to this anthology of verse provides valuable insights into Sheers' thoughts and feelings about landscape and its impact on poets.

—— (2009) *A Poet's Guide to Britain*, Digital Classics (DVD). Originally broadcast by the BBC, this is an excellent guide to six poems inspired by the British landscape. While not directly connected with Skirrid Hill, this well-produced DVD offers interesting ideas about place and identity.

—— (2008) 'Poetry and place: some personal reflections', *Geography*, Vol. 93, Part 3. A useful article that outlines some of Sheers' ideas about poetry and landscape.

—— (2008) 'Shared territories, poetic landscapes' in *emagazine*, Issue 41 (September 2008). This useful article provides an introduction to the collection, and offers some personal insights into Sheers' creative process as well as comments on the title and connections between the poems.

—— (2007) *Resistance*, Faber. This is Sheers' Second World War novel that tells the story of what might have happened had there been a successful German occupation of Britain.

—— (2006) *Owen Sheers Reading from his Poems* (CD), The Poetry Archive. This is invaluable: Sheers introduces several of the poems and his readings bring the poems alive.

—— (2004) *The Dust Diaries*, Faber and Faber. This semi-fictional biography of Sheers' great-great-uncle, the missionary Arthur Cripps, is a beautifully written and fascinating story.

—— (2000) *The Blue Book*, Seren. Sheers' first collection, which contains touching family poems and some even scarier characters than *Skirrid Hill*'s Joseph Jones.

Reviews and articles on *Skirrid Hill*

Sarah Crown in the *Guardian*, 25 February 2006. This is a perceptive and analytical review that praises the collection: **http://tinyurl.com/4o4jwmv**.

Carrie Etter in *New Welsh Review*, No. 72, Summer 2006. This acerbic review quibbles about some uses of metaphor, but praises the immediacy of poems such as 'Hedge School'. Available at **www.poetrymagazines.org.uk/magazine/record.asp?id=19349**.

Luke McBratney, 'A View of *Skirrid Hill*' in *The English Review*, Vol. 21, No.3, February 2011.

Anira Rowenchild, 'The Presence of the Past: Gillian Clarke and Owen Sheers' in *The English Review*, Vol. 22, No. 3, February 2012. If you have access to the *English Review* online archive, you may also download teaching notes to accompany this article.

On poetry

Lennard, J. (2005) *The Poetry Handbook: a guide to reading poetry for pleasure and practical criticism*, Oxford University Press.

Preminger, A. and Brogan, T. V. F. (1993) *The New Princeton Encyclopedia of Poetry and Poetics*, Princeton University Press.

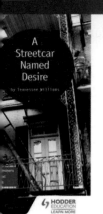